Fondue

Fondue

Great Food to Dip, Dunk, Savor, and Swirl

Rick Rodgers

William Morrow and Company, Inc. / New York

It is the policy of William Morrow and Company, Inc., and its imprints and affiliates, recognizing the importance of preserving what has been written, to print the books we publish on acid-free paper, and we exert our best efforts to that end.

Library of Congress Cataloging-in-Publication Data
Rodgers, Rick, 1953–
    Fondue : great food to dip, dunk, savor, and swirl / Rick Rodgers.
        p.   cm.
    Includes index.
    ISBN 0-06-088917-9
    1. Fondue.   I. Title.
TX825.R76   1998
641.8'1—dc21   97-38058
                                                     CIP

Printed in the United States of America

BOOK DESIGN BY RICHARD ORIOLO

Acknowledgments

Sharing a fondue meal is one of the most fun ways to eat. It is only appropriate that I had a great time working on this book, helped along by good friends in the kitchen. Judith Dunbar Hines and I met when she was the administrator of a cooking school, and we've been swapping recipes and industry gossip ever since. Steven Evasew and I went to culinary school together, then Steve joined me in my catering business—once we got past our first cocktail party for five hundred guests and didn't kill each other in the process, we knew we would be lifelong friends. These two cohorts brought talent, good humor, and calm, along with their knives and aprons, to my kitchen. Thanks also to Barbara Rupp for helping with research.

At William Morrow, I am very grateful to my editors, Jennifer Kaye and Pam Hoenig, for initiating this project, book designer Richard Oriolo for making it so attractive to the eye, and copyeditor Carole Berglie for watching out for my grammatical glitches. And a final tip of the hat to my agent, Susan Ginsburg, and her assistant, John Hodgman.

Contents

Fearless Fried Fondue   57

The Asian Hot Pot Family   93

Dessert from a Pot 127

The World of Fondue

FONDUE is fun. Fondue is romantic. Fondue is sweet or savory. Fondue is easy to make. It can be exotic with Asian flavors or as comforting as melted cheese.

A new generation is discovering the pleasures of fondue. Like a movie star of a certain age, fondue made a big splash, went into retirement, and is now making a comeback with a vengeance. But the culinary world has changed since fondue's first appearance. New ingredients and flavors have exploded across the food world map. Roast garlic, pesto, chiles, lemongrass, balsamic vinegar, fresh ginger, sun-dried tomatoes, goat cheese, mascarpone, and espresso have incorporated themselves into our national palate. I have tossed these exciting flavors into the fondue pot with mouthwatering results. Old favorites are revisited, too.

Fondue is part of my family's heritage. It is a Swiss invention, and my grandmother was born in Liechtenstein, a tiny principality next door, less than an hour from Zurich. While I can't say that I have memories of Grandma standing over the stove stirring up a batch of fondue, I recall that when it first became popular with Americans in the sixties, she remarked that it was nothing new to her. When I visited my family in Liechtenstein for the first time in the 1980s, we celebrated with a fondue dinner on a boat that paddled around Lake Zurich.

Yes, fondue is easy to make, but for most people it is an indulgence. The three most familiar types of fondue (cheese, fried, and chocolate) are admittedly not for calorie or fat gram counters. But fondue is a "feel good" food. (For cooks who want low-fat fondue, one of the Asian hot pots, where the food is simmered in broth, is the way to go, but I'll bet they want chocolate fondue for dessert.) When you have a special occasion that calls for an intimate meal with close friends, take out the fondue pot and make a fast, fun feast.

Equipment

There are two basic fondue pots: one for cheese fondue and another for fried fondue. Fondue pots come with burner units fueled by alcohol, fuel paste, or even electricity. Cheese fondue

pots should be made of a material that diffuses the heat, preferably ceramic or earthenware. Fried fondues are best prepared in metal pots that absorb the heat and keep the cooking oil hot. If you like to make both kinds of fondue, you need both kinds of pots. Asian hot pots are more elaborate in design, but a metal fondue pot that keeps the broth simmering can be substituted. For dessert fondues, a ceramic or earthenware cheese fondue pot is the best bet, but keep the flame very low so the chocolate doesn't scorch. One of my favorite fondue sets comes with both ceramic and metal pots. Best of all, water can be simmered in the metal pot with the ceramic pot fitted inside to act as a double boiler. This setup protects delicate fondues that are made with goat cheese or chocolate. Electric pots are very practical and versatile. Details on the different kinds of pots are outlined in the "Equipment" section that opens each chapter.

Fondue forks are an important part of the ritual. If possible, buy forks with identifying marks, such as different colored handles, so guests can tell which fork is theirs. The forks can get hot, especially in hot oil, so warn your guests or provide an extra fork for transferring the food to the mouth. Asian hot pots usually come with tiny wire baskets for dunking and cooking the food, but they may have to be purchased separately.

Heating the Pot

Most fondue pots are very well designed to avoid any accidental tipping, but it's a good idea to be sure the pot sits securely on its stand before making a purchase. Fondue pots are most often heated by a wick-type burning unit filled with denatured alcohol or a compartment that holds a can or container of fuel paste.

Denatured alcohol makes the hottest flame and won't smoke while burning. The flame can be controlled by adjusting the flue that covers the unit. A filled unit with a low flame (for cheese fondue) will burn for about 2 hours; larger flames (for oil fondues) will last about 1 hour. Don't substitute lamp fuel, which doesn't burn as hot and is often perfumed as well. Denatured alcohol is available at hardware stores, but try to purchase a can with a spigot top—it will make the chore of filling the receptacle much easier.

Fuel paste, such as Sterno, comes in squat cans or in foil containers. The cans are the easiest to find, available in every hardware store and many supermarkets. However, some burner units are shaped to hold a shallow container of fuel paste, which can be difficult to locate. Look for them in well-stocked kitchenware stores.

Serving Fondue

Fondue is meant to be an intimate meal. It can be a very romantic dinner for two, or a casual supper for four to six. Six is the maximum amount of people per pot. The logistics of more than six people trying to dunk dinner is clear. But with fried fondues, the problem changes—with more than six pieces of meat cooking at the same time in the oil, the oil temperature will reduce and the food won't cook properly.

The fondue pot should be placed in the center of the table, within easy reach of all the guests. It is a good idea to cover the table with a tablecloth, and to be sure the fondue pot doesn't burn the table, set it on a lazy Susan, cutting board, or large trivet.

The dipping ingredients should be arranged as beautifully

and artistically as possible, adding drama and color to the fondue ritual. Nestle florets of vegetables into a basket, garnished with tufts of curly green kale. Line a platter with lemon leaves (available at florists) before arranging the food on top. Tuck bunches of fresh herbs from the garden between the mounds of food. Or garnish the platter in the Chinese fashion by scattering flower blossoms over the ingredients—just be sure that the flowers are unsprayed and nonpoisonous. Good choices are chrysanthemums, violets, roses, and nasturtiums. And, of course, line the bread cube basket with a crisp, clean napkin.

In Switzerland, the preferred beverages for a fondue meal are hot tea or shots of kirsch. My cousins were shocked at the "unhealthy" idea of topping off the warm fondue in my tummy with cold wine, warning me that I was courting sure gastronomic disaster. They insisted that I drink something hot, or at least room temperature. Their reasoning was sincere, but not well founded. The best suggestion is to drink more of the same wine that the fondue was made with, such as dry white wine, hard cider, beer, or apple juice.

Cheese Fondue: Warm and Wonderful

WHEN most people think of fondue, it is the classic Swiss cheese version that comes to mind (and makes our mouths water). There are many reasons for its appeal. First of all, it's fun to make and the method of eating guarantees camaraderie among all the diners—it's almost impossible to be mad at someone you're eating with while dunking and swirling the bread in something that tastes so good.

No one knows who "invented" fondue. Some food historians believe it developed when the Swiss created a cheese sauce to soften stale bread during a siege. Others believe it evolved from the farmhouse method of cooking Raclette cheese, another fine Swiss contribution to cheese culture. This involves heating a wedge of Raclette in front of a fireplace until it melts, and scraping the warm, soft cheese onto boiled potatoes or bread. Regardless of the source, fondue has traveled out of Switzerland and spread all over the world. And as other countries come to know and love fondue, other local cheeses have found themselves cooked into luscious fondues.

In the last few years, Americans have developed a taste for good cheese. Local dairies are making excellent cheeses that rival European versions. However, not all cheeses make it into the Fondue Hall of Fame. Many cheeses just don't melt smoothly, and make a stringy, tough, or gritty fondue. While I have tried to use as many cheeses as possible, if one of your favorites isn't here, it could be that it just is better uncooked than melted.

Equipment

The traditional Swiss cheese fondue pot is called a *caquelon*. It is made of ceramic or earthenware and shaped like a deep skillet. The thick pottery diffuses the heat and discourages the fondue from scorching. Metal fondue pots absorb the heat, and cheese fondues burn quickly in them—they are best saved for deep-fried meat fondues. Any ceramic, earthenware, or enameled cast-iron casserole will work as a fondue pot, but be sure it sits securely on the burner, which can be improvised from a hot plate. Of course, electric fondue pots are also an option.

Use an extension cord, if needed, to safely plug in the pot and avoid an accident.

Ingredients

Wine and Other Alcoholic Beverages: Wine for fondue should be crisp and slightly tart, as the acidity reacts with the proteins and fats in the cheese to make a smoother fondue. Most recipes include some kind of acid (such as lemon juice or vinegar) to ensure this reaction takes place. As in all good cooking, the better the wine, the better your dish, but this is doubly true with fondue. A moderately priced California Sauvignon Blanc is my first choice, but other dry, light-bodied white wines, and even Champagne, can be used. Chardonnay is too heavy-bodied to be a good fondue wine. Only a couple of recipes use red wine, as the color of the fondue will not be to everyone's liking, although it is easy to camouflage with chopped herbs.

Some fondues begin with hard apple cider or beer. Hard apple cider is not apple juice—it is alcoholic and not nearly as sweet. Well-stocked liquor stores carry it, especially now that it is being produced by quite a few American microbreweries. When choosing beer to make fondue, pick a light-flavored (but not "lite") lager or ale—dark beers and heavy stouts will overpower the flavor of the cheese.

Kirsch and Other Hard Liquors: If you are an accomplished baker, you probably own a bottle of kirsch, as it flavors many classic European desserts. This cherry *eau-de-vie* is sometimes labeled *kirschwasser*, which means "cherry water." It is worth buying a fine imported kirsch, as some cheaper domestic brands can be more firewater than cherry water. Excellent kirsch is always expensive; it takes pounds and pounds of cherries to distill into a liter of kirsch. If you don't want to make this investment (remember it will last for years), use a good Cognac or brandy instead.

The Bread Basket: There is more to the fondue bread basket than cubes of French or Italian bread. Swiss bread bakers are among the best in the world. Every bakery makes its own "farmer's bread," a mixed-grain, slightly sour loaf with a firm, chewy interior and crisp crust. While some Swiss restaurants will serve fondue with the familiar French-style baguette, home cooks often prefer their national daily loaf. If you have a good baker or natural food store nearby that makes this kind of bread, serve it with baguette cubes to add variety to your dipping ingredient selection. Other breads make good fondue dippers—pita and English muffins (cut into wedges), focaccia and breadsticks, croissants and pumpernickel.

The bread shouldn't be stale, but it should be firm. Cut the bread just before serving so it doesn't dry out. If you want to cube it ahead of time, wrap the cubes in foil or a waxed paper–lined bakery bag—a plastic bag will soften the crust. The cubes should be bite-sized, no longer than 1 inch square, with a piece of crust on each cube to help secure it onto the fondue fork.

Cornstarch and Flour: These two ingredients act as binders, knitting together the liquid and semi-solid components in the melted cheese. However, they reach their full binding power only when brought to a boil, so don't judge a fondue's thickness until it reaches the boiling point.

Cheeses: Cheese is, of course, fondue's raison d'être. Support your local cheese store. Fine cheese is a living thing, and should be handled with a professional's care. It is always better to buy your cheese freshly cut than pre-cut and wrapped. If you are experimenting with your own fondue recipes, remember that some cheeses melt better than others.

All of the weights in the recipes' ingredient lists are for untrimmed cheese—in other words, the amount that you need to buy. The volume (cup) measurement is for the approximate amount after the cheese has been trimmed, if necessary, and shredded or cubed.

Here is a glossary of the cheeses used in this book:

Appenzeller: Semi-hard Swiss cheese with a sharp tang. Used in combination with Emmentaler and Gruyère in the classic Swiss fondue mixture.

Brie: Soft cheese with an edible white rind. Imported French Brie is much preferred to the domestic variety. When you purchase Brie, it should have a soft, but not runny, consistency—once a wheel of Brie is cut, it will not ripen further, so if you buy a hard, underripe piece, it will stay that way. To use Brie for fondue, the rind must be trimmed, which is easiest to do if the cheese is well chilled.

Cheddar: True Cheddar is one of the glories of Britain—sharp, crumbly, its rind blossoming from the cloth that wraps the cheese wheel. It is usually not colored, and has a strawlike hue. Domestic Cheddar can be very good, especially if you buy from a small cooperative dairy. Of course, British Cheddar is more expensive, and while it makes superior fondue, most Americans will choose a good domestic Cheddar.

Cheddar, Smoked: Some dairies make smoked Cheddar, which comes in 8- or 16-ounce wax-covered blocks. Of course, remove the wax coating before shredding.

Chèvre: Chèvre refers to an entire category of goat cheese (except goat Feta cheese). They come in a huge variety of shapes—some have rinds, some are coated in herbs, spices, or even wood ash, some are aged and hard, and some are young and soft. There are fine French and domestic goat cheeses. For fondue, use a young, soft, white goat cheese without any seasonings, preferably a log shape from a local source (I buy my favorite brand from a stand at my neighborhood farmer's market). If you use a factory-made cheese, such as Boucheron, remove the thin white rind. Take extra care not to overheat chèvre, or it will turn grainy.

Cream Cheese: I use Philadelphia Brand cream cheese. There are some gum-free brands, but the gum in "Philly" is harmless and helps the cheese melt more smoothly.

Domestic Swiss: Domestic Swiss cheese is not as fully matured as the classic Emmentaler, but it still can be used for fondue.

Edam: A ball-shaped Holland cheese, coated with red wax (exported Edam and Gouda cheeses are covered with wax, yet sold uncoated in the Netherlands). It has a mild flavor that takes well to embellishments. When used for a fondue, it should be finely chopped, not shredded.

Emmentaler: The Swiss cheese, with holes of various shapes occurring throughout the wheel, caused by carbon dioxide forming as the cheese ages. There is also an excellent French version, but it is more expensive.

Explorateur: A creamy cheese from the triple-crème family. The white rind can be eaten when the cheese is served by itself, but must be removed for fondue making. Chill the cheese well before trimming.

Fontina, Italian: Italian Fontina d'Aosta is a raw milk cheese from Italy's Piedmont region. In my opinion, it is one of the world's great cheeses. Scandinavian (usually Swedish) Fontina is a pale imitation.

Gorgonzola: A classic blue-veined cheese from Italy that comes in two versions. *Dolce,* which means "sweet," is the younger, with a soft texture and mildly assertive flavor. *Naturale* is aged and stronger in aroma and flavor. For fondue, use the *dolce.*

Gouda: Another famous Holland cheese, but also one with a neutral flavor that benefits from seasoning. Americans are most familiar with the red paraffin–covered young, semi-soft version. Aged Gouda, dark-gold color with a firm texture, is sharper. It doesn't melt well enough on its own and must be combined with younger Gouda to make a successful fondue.

Gruyère: Real Gruyère cheese is Swiss-made from raw milk, with pea-sized holes, and has a rich, full flavor. French Gruyère (often called Comté) is also an excellent fondue cheese.

Kasseri: A semi-hard, sharp Greek cheese that is available at Greek delicatessens and many cheese stores.

Manchego: With its mildly sharp tang and flaky texture, sheep's milk Spanish Manchego reminds some people of British Cheddar. Found at well-stocked cheese stores, it is a fine melting cheese and makes an excellent fondue.

Mascarpone: Mascarpone is not really a cheese, but actually a type of clotted cream with a very thick body and mellow, sweet flavor. It is very perishable, owing to its low sodium content. I am lucky enough to live in an Italian neighborhood where the dairy shops make their own mascarpone, but most mascarpone is imported. Recently, thanks to the popularity of tiramisù, domestic Mascarpone has been appearing in super-markets, but it is usually as expensive as the Italian version.

Monterey Jack: A good, mild melting cheese available at every supermarket.

Mozzarella: Fresh Mozzarella, shaped into balls and stored in brine, is wonderful, but it doesn't melt well. For the fondue recipes in this book, use a good packaged supermarket variety.

Parmigiano-Reggiano: This glorious grating cheese is sometimes referred to simply as "Parmesan cheese." As many countries make Parmesan cheese, and much of that is terrible, I like to make the distinction. Parmigiano-Reggiano comes from Parma, not Wisconsin or Argentina. Never purchase grated Parmigiano, as it gets stale very quickly. Get in the habit of purchasing it by the wedge and grating it as needed.

Provolone, Aged: Provolone is a sharp-tasting Italian slic-ing cheese. Aged Provolone has the most flavor and is the choice for fondue. For the best results, mix it with other good-melting cheeses.

Preparing Vegetables for Dipping: Some vegeta-bles are fine raw, but others benefit from a quick boil to set their color or make them less crunchy. Dipping vegetables that are best when blanched first include asparagus, broccoli, car-rots, cauliflower, and chayote.

Cut the vegetables into their desired shape (florets, spears, or sticks). Bring a large pot of lightly salted water to a boil over high heat. In separate batches, cook the vegetables just until crisp-tender, usually no longer than 2 minutes. Drain in a colander and rinse well under cold running water to stop the cooking and set the color. (If you are cooking a number of vegetables, transfer the vegetables from the water to the colander with a skimmer or large slotted spoon, and keep the water boiling. Start with the most mild-tasting vegetable first, as the vegetables will leech some flavor into the cooking water.) Pat the drained vegetables dry with paper towels, and refrigerate in plastic bags until ready to serve.

Making and Serving Cheese Fondue

Cheese fondue is usually served with cubes of bread, a green salad, and a beverage. To turn it into a heartier meal, serve a wider range of accompaniments. Why not offer cubes of cooked meat or poultry to dip into the fondue, vegetables, or even fruits? The variety of dipping ingredients will make a more substantial offering than a basket of bread cubes.

Fondue is most easily prepared in a saucepan on the kitchen stove, then transferred to a fondue pot for serving. While some cooks enjoy the showiness of mixing the fondue at the table, I think it's a hassle, and the tabletop burners are rarely strong enough to do any actual cooking. If you wish, prepare the fondue on the stove in its ceramic or earthenware fondue pot, but use a flame diffuser to keep the pot from cracking.

Provide each diner with a plate and a fondue fork. Some guests may appreciate an extra napkin to use as a bib. If you are serving a green salad, place a separate salad fork at each place setting.

Regardless of how the basic ingredients may change, the procedure for making cheese fondue is constant. A liquid (such as wine, beer, cider, or broth) is heated just to simmering—letting the liquid come to a boil at this point often adversely changes the flavor. The trimmed, shredded, or cubed cheese is tossed with cornstarch or flour, and gradually stirred into the simmering liquid. Melting the cheese gradually encourages a smooth fondue. Stir constantly throughout the melting period, reaching the bottom and corners of the pot. The fondue should come to a gentle boil to allow the starch to cook completely and do its job as a binder, but only for a few seconds, or the fondue may curdle. A shot of hard liquor is often added as a finishing touch. (The Swiss believe that the liquor helps make the fondue more digestible, but it is really a matter of seasoning.) If the fondue was made in a saucepan, transfer it to a warmed fondue pot (fill the pot with hot tap water for a few minutes, then toss out the water and dry the pot) and place over a low burner, where it should remain warm with a gentle bubbling throughout the meal.

Here are a few troubleshooting tips:

- If the fondue is too thin, and you have leftover shredded cheese, stir about 1 cup of the cheese into the fondue. Or dissolve 1 tablespoon of cornstarch in 1 tablespoon of the cooking liquid, and gradually stir enough of the mixture into the simmering fondue for it to reach the desired consistency.

- If the fondue is too thick, just add more of the cooking liquid, warmed first in a small saucepan or a microwave oven.

- If the fondue is lumpy or gritty, briskly whisk in 1 tablespoon of fresh lemon juice or vinegar.

Fondue Great Food to Dip, Dunk, Savor, and Swirl

- If the fondue separates, return it to the kitchen stove and reheat over medium heat, whisking constantly. If the fondue is mixed well by guests as they dip, this shouldn't happen.

The guests should spear a bite-sized cube of bread (or meat or a vegetable) onto their fondue forks and swirl it into the fondue. Tell your guest to give the fondue a good "figure eight" swirl with their forks as they dip (to discourage the fondue separating) and to occasionally scrape the bottom of the pot with their bread (to keep the bottom from burning). In Switzerland, there are "punishments" for the careless guests who lose their bread in fondue: a man has to buy the next pot of fondue or a bottle of wine (assuming the dining is in a restaurant), and a woman is supposed to kiss a man of her choice.

Resist the temptation to wipe every last drop of fondue out of the pot, and leave a thin film in the bottom to cook into a golden brown crust. Let the crust cool, then pry it out of the pot and divide among the participants. This morsel is called *la religieuse* or *la croûte*, and while not a religious experience, it is pretty darned good.

Classic Swiss Three-Cheese Fondue

makes 4 to 6 servings

SWISS CHEESE SHOPS combine different shredded cheeses to make their own proprietary fondue mixes. This version uses three of Switzerland's greatest cheeses: Gruyère for its full flavor, Emmentaler for nuttiness, and Appenzeller for sharpness. If you can get only one or two of these cheeses, don't worry—use about 1 pound (trimmed weight) of whatever you can get, and make your own house blend. It will still be delicious.

1 garlic clove, peeled

1 cup dry white wine

1 tablespoon fresh lemon juice

8 ounces Gruyère cheese, rind
   trimmed and discarded, and
   shredded (about 2½ cups)

8 ounces Emmentaler cheese,
   rind trimmed and dis-
   carded, and shredded
   (about 2½ cups)

3 ounces Appenzeller cheese,
   cut into small cubes (about ½ cup)

4 teaspoons cornstarch

1 tablespoon kirsch

A few gratings of fresh nutmeg

Freshly ground pepper, to taste

What to Dip

Crusty mixed grain bread, French or Italian bread, cut into bite-sized cubes (leave a piece of crust on each cube) • Cooked chicken breast, skin and bone removed, cut into bite-sized cubes • Cooked garlic sausage or knock-wurst, cut into bite-sized wedges • Boiled new potatoes • Asparagus spears, broccoli florets, or cauliflower florets, prepared for dipping (see page 14)

Fondue Great Food to Dip, Dunk, Savor, and Swirl

1. Rub the inside of a medium, heavy-bottomed saucepan with the garlic; discard the garlic. Add the wine and lemon juice and bring to a bare simmer over medium heat.

2. In a medium bowl, toss the Gruyère, Emmentaler, and Appenzeller cheeses with the cornstarch. A handful at a time, stir the cheese mixture into the wine, stirring the first batch until it is almost completely melted before adding another. The fondue can bubble gently, but do not boil. Stir in the kirsch and season with the nutmeg and pepper.

3. Transfer to a cheese fondue pot and keep warm over a fondue burner. Serve immediately, with dipping ingredients of your choice.

French Gruyère Fondue: Substitute an additional 11 ounces Gruyère cheese, rind trimmed and removed and shredded (about 3¼ cups) for the Emmentaler and Appenzeller cheeses, and Cognac or brandy for the kirsch.

Fondue Dijonnaise: Stir 1½ tablespoons Dijon mustard into the fondue. Substitute Cognac or brandy for the kirsch.

American Swiss Cheese Fondue: Domestic Swiss cheese is not as fully matured as imported Swiss cheese, but it can make a fine fondue. Substitute 1 pound domestic Swiss cheese, cut into tiny cubes, finely shredded, for the Gruyère, Emmenthaler, and Appenzeller cheeses.

Wine-Free Fondue: Substitute ½ cup chicken stock, preferably homemade, and ½ cup milk for the wine. Do not add the lemon juice until the chicken stock and milk have come to a simmer.

Brie and Pesto Fondue

A PLATTER WITH a wheel of baked brie is one of those dishes that says "Party!" Its smooth, melting texture inspired this fragrant fondue, aromatic with fresh basil. Try it as a supper dish with cubes of cooked chicken breast.

What to Dip

Crusty French or Italian bread, cut into bite-sized cubes (leave a piece of crust on each cube) • Croissants, cut into bite-sized cubes • Cooked chicken breast, skin and bone removed, cut into bite-sized cubes • Asparagus spears, broccoli florets, or cauliflower florets, prepared for dipping (see page 14) • Cherry tomatoes

¼ cup packed, coarsely chopped fresh basil leaves

1 ounce freshly grated Parmigiano-Reggiano cheese (¼ cup)

1 garlic clove, minced

1 cup dry white wine

1 tablespoon white wine vinegar

1 pound ripe Brie cheese, well chilled, rind trimmed and discarded, cut into small cubes (about 2 cups)

2 tablespoons cornstarch

Freshly ground pepper, to taste

1. Place the basil, Parmigiano-Reggiano cheese, and garlic in a blender. With the machine running, add ¼ cup of the wine and process until thick. Set the pesto aside.

2. In a medium, heavy-bottomed saucepan, bring the remaining ¾ cup wine and the vinegar to a bare simmer over medium heat. In a medium bowl, toss the Brie cheese with the corn-

starch. A handful at a time, stir the cheese into the saucepan, stirring the first batch until melted before adding another. Allow the fondue to bubble once or twice, but do not boil. Stir in the pesto and season with the pepper.

3. Transfer to a cheese fondue pot and keep warm over a fondue burner. Serve immediately, with dipping ingredients of your choice.

Welsh Cheddar and Bacon Rabbit Fondue

makes 6 to 8 servings

WHEN I HAVE weekend houseguests, this is one of my favorite things to serve for breakfast or brunch. The citizens of the British Isles are bonkers for breakfast, and hot Cheddar rabbit spooned over toast and bacon is right up there with their beloved bangers and kippers. Rabbit is actually a cheese sauce, and supposedly got its name because cheese was as common to a Welsh kitchen as the rabbits were ubiquitous in the fields. Some cooks felt that "rabbit" was much too coarse a name for a sauce (and confusing, to boot), and tried to change it to "rarebit." Although some cookbooks use the upgraded term, "rabbit" is the original.

What to Dip

Toasted English muffins, cut into wedges •
Assorted apples and pears, cut into slices

6 slices of bacon

1 cup ale or lager beer

1 pound extra-sharp Cheddar cheese, shredded
   (about 6 cups)

1½ tablespoons all-purpose flour

2 teaspoons dry mustard, preferably English

1 tablespoon Worcestershire sauce

Freshly ground pepper, to taste

1. Place the bacon in a cold, large skillet. Cook over medium heat until crisp and brown, about 5 minutes. Transfer the bacon to paper towels to drain and cool. Finely chop the bacon.

2. In a medium, heavy-bottomed saucepan, bring the ale to a bare simmer over medium heat. In a medium bowl, toss the cheese with the flour. Gradually stir the cheese into the saucepan, stirring the first batch until melted before adding another. In a small bowl, dissolve the mustard in the Worcestershire sauce. Stir into the fondue, along with the chopped bacon. Allow the fondue to come to a bare simmer, but do not boil. Season generously with the pepper.

3. Transfer to a cheese fondue pot and keep warm over a fondue burner. Serve immediately, with dipping ingredients of your choice.

Welsh Rarebit with Shrimp: Add ½ pound cooked, peeled, and finely chopped shrimp.

Gingered Curry and Cheddar Fondue

MY MULTIETHNIC NEIGHBORHOOD is a constant source of inspiration, and I make some of my best culinary discoveries at the Indian grocery store. For example, there are a number of interesting, delicious Indian breads that make excellent dippers for this mildly spiced curry fondue. Two of my favorites are pappadums (thin lentil flour, tortilla-like wafers, available plain or spiced, fried at home until crispy) and naan (somewhat like a thick pita). This recipe illustrates one of my favorite cooking tips. When a recipe calls for minced fresh ginger, there's no need to peel the ginger or even actually chop it. Instead, I shred it on the large holes of a cheese grater. This not only gives a finer texture than chopping but leaves most of the tough fibers behind, still attached to the knob.

2 tablespoons unsalted butter

1 medium onion, finely chopped

1 medium celery rib with leaves, finely chopped

2 tablespoons shredded fresh ginger (see above)

1 garlic clove, minced

2 teaspoons Madras-style curry powder

1 cup lager beer

What to Dip

Fried Indian pappadums (recipe follows) • Indian naan or pita bread, split, toasted, and cut into wedges • Cooked chicken breast, skinned and boned, cut into cubes • Cooked shrimp, peeled and deveined • Asparagus spears, prepared for dipping (see page 14)

1 pound extra-sharp Cheddar cheese, shredded
   (about 6 cups)
1 tablespoon plus 2 teaspoons cornstarch
2 tablespoons chopped mango chutney (see Note)

1. In a medium, heavy-bottomed saucepan, heat the butter over medium heat. Add the onion, celery, ginger, and garlic. Cook, stirring occasionally, until the onion is golden, about 5 minutes. Add the curry and stir until fragrant, about 30 seconds. Stir in the beer and bring to a simmer.

2. In a medium bowl, toss the cheese with the cornstarch. A handful at a time, stir the cheese into the saucepan, stirring the first batch until melted before adding another. Stir in the chutney. Allow the fondue to come to a bare simmer, but do not boil.

3. Transfer to a cheese fondue pot and keep warm over a fondue burner. Serve immediately, with dipping ingredients of your choice.

Fried Pappadums: In a large skillet, over medium-high heat, heat enough vegetable oil to come ½ inch up the sides of the pan until very hot, but not smoking. One at a time, fry the pappadums in the oil—they will crisp and puff slightly almost immediately. Transfer to paper towels to drain. Cool completely.

Note: Mango chutney is often labeled "Major Grey's Chutney." To chop chutney, remove one or two solid pieces of mango from the jar, mince finely on a chopping board, transfer to a small bowl, and mix with enough syrup to make 2 tablespoons.

Cheddar, Roast Garlic, and Zinfandel Fondue

makes 4 to 6 servings

IN RECENT YEARS, roast garlic has become a staple in many cooks' kitchens, and rightfully so. Roasting mellows the garlic and adds a caramelized flavor. Matched with equally assertive ingredients like extra-sharp Cheddar cheese and Zinfandel, this is a fondue to share with friends who like food that packs a punch.

> **What to Dip**
>
> Crusty French or Italian bread, cut into cubes (leave a piece of crust on each cube) • Smoked sausage, cut into wedges • Raw red bell pepper slices

    1 cup Zinfandel wine, or other hearty red wine

    1 tablespoon red wine vinegar

12 ounces extra-sharp Cheddar cheese, shredded (about 4½ cups)

2 ounces freshly grated Parmigiano-Reggiano cheese (½ cup)

1 tablespoon cornstarch

¼ cup Roast Garlic Purée (recipe follows)

¼ teaspoon crushed hot red pepper flakes

1. In a medium, heavy-bottomed saucepan, bring the wine and vinegar to a bare simmer over medium heat.

2. In a medium bowl, toss the Cheddar and Parmigiano-Reggiano cheeses with the cornstarch. A handful at a time, stir the cheeses into the saucepan, stirring the first batch until melted before adding another. Stir in the roasted garlic. Season with the hot pepper flakes.

Fondue Great Food to Dip, Dunk, Savor, and Swirl

3. Transfer to a cheese fondue pot and keep warm over a fondue burner. Serve immediately, with dipping ingredients of your choice.

Roast Garlic Purée: Position a rack in the center of the oven and preheat to 400°F. Cut 2 large, plump garlic heads in half through their equators, trying to keep the cloves as intact as possible. Drizzle about 1 teaspoon extra-virgin olive oil over the cut surfaces. Put the two halves of each garlic head back together to reform each head in its original shape. Wrap each head in aluminum foil. Bake until the garlic is softened and the cloves are deep beige (open the foil to check), 40 to 50 minutes, depending on the size of the garlic. Unwrap and cool completely. Squeeze the softened garlic cloves out of their hulls into a small bowl, discarding the hulls. Using a fork, mash the roasted garlic until smooth. Use as a seasoning for fondues, whisk into salad dressings, or spread onto bread. Makes about ⅓ cup.

Smoky Cheddar and Apple Cider Fondue

makes 4 to 6 servings

APPLE CIDER AND Cheddar cheese are a wonderful pair and create a sensational fondue for cool autumn evenings. Hard cider (don't confuse it with regular apple cider) is one of my favorite alcoholic beverages. Semi-dry, often with a slight effervescence, it is very easy to quaff, and equally easy to lose track of just how many glasses you've downed. Formerly available only as French or British imports, a few American cider presses are jumping onto the apple cart, and excellent domestic brands can be found in well-stocked liquor stores. I like to serve this with an assortment of apples from the farmer's market—red, green, sweet, tart, crisp, and tender.

What to Dip

Pumpernickel or rye bread, cut into bite-sized cubes (leave a piece of crust on each cube) • Cooked smoked sausage, such as kielbasa, cut into bite-sized wedges • An assortment of apples, cored and sliced, tossed with fresh lemon juice to discourage discoloring

1 cup hard apple cider or ½ cup
    nonalcoholic apple cider and
    ½ cup dry white wine
1 tablespoon fresh lemon juice
1 pound smoked Cheddar
    cheese, shredded
    (about 6 cups)
1 tablespoon plus 1 teaspoon cornstarch
3 tablespoons high-quality apple butter
    (made from only apples and cider)
A few gratings of fresh nutmeg
Freshly ground pepper, to taste

1. In a medium, heavy-bottomed saucepan, heat the cider and lemon juice over medium heat until barely simmering.

2. In a medium bowl, toss the cheese with the cornstarch. A handful at a time, stir the cheese into the saucepan, stirring the first batch until melted before adding another. Stir in the apple butter, and season with the nutmeg and pepper.

3. Transfer to a cheese fondue pot and keep warm over a fondue burner. Serve immediately, with dipping ingredients of your choice.

Chèvre and Fresh Herb
Fondue

makes 4 to 6 servings

W HEN FONDUE HAD its first wave of popularity back in the 1960s, very few Americans had ever tasted goat cheese. Now, chèvre is essential to new American cooking. In testing, I tried to make a fondue that used only goat cheese, but as the flavor was too intense when heated, cream cheese was added to tone down the sharpness. The result is a smooth, elegant, and very rich fondue perfect for serving with a chilled Chardonnay. Overheating will make the goat cheese grainy, so gentle cooking in a double boiler is important. Further protect the fondue from direct heat by serving from a chafing dish, or replacing the fondue burner with a votive candle.

What to Dip

Crusty French or Italian bread, cut into bite-sized cubes (leave a piece of crust on each cube) • Cooked chicken breast, skinless and boneless, cut into bite-sized cubes • Broccoli or cauliflower florets, prepared for dipping (see page 14) • Raw red bell pepper slices • Raw celery sticks • Raw zucchini slices

1 cup heavy cream

1 garlic clove, crushed through
    a press

8 ounces cream cheese, cut into
    small cubes, at room
    temperature

8 ounces rindless chèvre (goat cheese), crumbled with a
    fork, at room temperature

1 tablespoon plus 1 teaspoon cornstarch

1 tablespoon fresh lemon juice

1 tablespoon minced fresh basil

1 tablespoon minced fresh chives

1 teaspoon minced fresh tarragon

1 teaspoon minced fresh parsley

Freshly ground pepper, to taste

1. In a small saucepan or a microwave oven, heat the cream and garlic over medium heat until bubbles appear around the edges of the cream. Transfer to the top part of a double boiler set over simmering water.

2. Gradually add the cream cheese to the hot cream, whisking until smooth. In a medium bowl, toss the chèvre with the cornstarch. Gradually whisk in the chèvre mixture until smooth. Stir in the lemon juice, basil, chives, tarragon, and parsley. Season with the pepper.

3. Transfer to a chafing dish and keep warm over hot water (or serve in a cheese fondue pot kept warm by a votive candle). Serve immediately, with the dipping ingredients of your choice.

Caribbean Edam and Habanero Chile Fondue

makes 4 to 6 servings

EDAM CHEESE WAS introduced to the Caribbean islands by Dutch traders in Curaçao, and its popularity has spread from island to island. Many Caribbean dishes, especially Cuban and Puerto Rican, start with *sofrito,* a seasoning mixture of onions, ham, peppers, and garlic—a bold accent to mild Edam. Habanero chiles have a distinctive flavor, but they are the hottest around and should be regarded with caution.

What to Dip

Crusty French or Italian bread, cut into bite-sized cubes (leave a piece of crust on each cube) • Boiled new potatoes • Raw red bell peppers, cut into strips • Chayote, peeled and cut into bite-sized cubes, prepared for dipping (see page 14) • Cherry tomatoes

2 tablespoons olive oil

4 ounces smoked ham, finely chopped

2 scallions, white and green parts, finely chopped

1 medium red bell pepper, seeded and finely chopped

2 teaspoons minced, seeded habanero chile, or use 1 jalapeño pepper, seeded and minced

1 garlic clove, minced

$^1/_2$ teaspoon dried oregano

$^1/_2$ teaspoon dried thyme

$^3/_4$ cup lager beer

1 tablespoon cider vinegar

1 pound Edam cheese, wax removed, finely chopped

1 tablespoon cornstarch

1. In a medium, heavy-bottomed saucepan, heat the oil over medium heat. Add the ham, scallions, red pepper, chile, and garlic. Cook, stirring often, until the onion is golden, about 5 minutes. Add the oregano and thyme and stir until fragrant, about 30 seconds. Add the beer and vinegar and bring just to a simmer.

2. Toss the cheese with the cornstarch. Stir in the cheese, a handful at a time, stirring the first batch until melted before adding another.

3. Transfer the fondue to a ceramic or enameled cast-iron fondue pot and keep warm over a fondue burner. Serve immediately, with dipping ingredients of your choice.

Italian Fontina and Porcini Fondue

makes 4 to 6 servings

IN ITALY'S PIEDMONT, you'll find *fonduta*, a luxurious Fontina cheese sauce, poured over polenta or toast points, and often served with shavings of fresh truffles. For an American fondue version, approximate the earthy flavor of truffles with equally wonderful dried porcini mushrooms. As a variation, leave out the mushroom mixture and top the Fontina fondue with a few drizzles of truffle-infused oil, found at many gourmet markets. A fine Italian Fontina, not its Scandinavian knock-off, is a must.

1 ounce dried porcini
    mushrooms, quickly rinsed
    under cold water
2 tablespoons unsalted butter
4 ounces fresh mushrooms,
    finely chopped
2 tablespoons chopped shallots
1 cup dry white wine
1 tablespoon white wine vinegar
1 pound Fontina d'Aosta cheese, rind removed, cut into
    small cubes (about 3 cups)
1 tablespoon cornstarch
Freshly ground pepper, to taste

What to Dip

Crusty French or Italian bread, cut into bite-sized cubes (leave a piece of crust on each cube) • Cooked shrimp, peeled and deveined • Cooked baby artichoke hearts • Asparagus spears, prepared for dipping (see page 14) • Raw fennel bulb, cut into sticks • Small mushroom caps • Boiled new potatoes

Fondue Great Food to Dip, Dunk, Savor, and Swirl

1. In a small bowl, cover the dried mushrooms with 1 cup boiling water. Let stand until the mushrooms soften, about 20 minutes. Lift the mushrooms out of the soaking water, rinse to remove any grit, and finely chop. Strain the soaking liquid through a paper towel–lined sieve into a bowl. Set the chopped porcini mushrooms and the strained liquid aside.

2. In a medium, heavy-bottomed saucepan, melt the butter over medium heat. Add the chopped fresh mushrooms and cook, stirring often, until they give off their liquid and begin to brown, about 5 minutes. Add the shallots and cook, stirring often, until they soften, about 1 minute. Add the strained soaking liquid and porcini mushrooms and bring to a boil over high heat. Cook until the liquid evaporates, about 5 minutes. Stir in the wine and vinegar and bring to a simmer.

3. Reduce the heat to medium. In a medium bowl, toss the cheese with the cornstarch. In three additions, stir the cheese into the saucepan, stirring until the first batch melts before adding another. Allow the fondue to come to a bare simmer, but do not boil. Season with the pepper.

4. Transfer the fondue to a cheese fondue pot and keep warm over a fondue burner. Serve immediately, with dipping ingredients of your choice.

Gorgonzola, Port, and Walnut Fondue

ORIGINALLY, I SERVED this fondue as a main course with cubes of roast beef tenderloin and vegetables, where it received rave reviews from blue cheese lovers. Now, as more fine American restaurants are offering cheese as a dessert course, I also serve it as a finale to a meal with glasses of the same port used in the fondue. No matter how you serve it, melted gorgonzola isn't very pretty—so serve it by candlelight and shrug off its not-so-lovely color.

What to Dip

Crusty French or Italian bread, cut into bite-sized cubes (leave a piece of crust on each cube) • Breadsticks • Roasted beef tenderloin, cut into cubes • Crisp, tart apples, such as Granny Smith, cut into slices, tossed with lemon juice to discourage browning • Firm ripe pears, such as Bosc, cut into slices

1 cup (4 ounces) walnuts

1 tablespoon unsalted butter

2 tablespoons minced shallots

⅓ cup plus 2 tablespoons tawny port

1 tablespoon fresh lemon juice

1 pound Gorgonzola cheese, trimmed (about 14 ounces)

2 tablespoons plus 1 teaspoon cornstarch

Freshly ground pepper, to taste

1. Position a rack in the top third of the oven and preheat to 350°F. Spread the walnuts out on a baking sheet. Bake, stirring occasionally, until the walnuts are fragrant and lightly toasted, 10 to 12 minutes. Cool completely. Finely chop the walnuts,

either in a food processor fitted with the metal chopping blade or by hand; set aside.

2. In a medium, heavy-bottomed saucepan, melt the butter over medium heat. Add the shallots and cook, stirring often, until softened, about 2 minutes. Add the port wine and lemon juice and bring to a bare simmer.

3. In a medium bowl, mash the Gorgonzola cheese with the cornstarch until well combined. In four or five additions, stir the cheese into the saucepan, stirring until the previous addition is melted before adding another. Allow the fondue to come to a bare simmer, but do not boil. Season with the pepper.

4. Transfer the fondue to a ceramic or enameled iron fondue pot and keep warm over a fondue burner. Serve immediately, with dipping ingredients of your choice and small bowls of the chopped walnuts, so guests can dip their fondue-covered food into the walnuts before eating.

Dutch Gouda and Beer Fondue

makes 4 to 6 servings

REGULAR GOUDA, WHICH can be found in even the most remote supermarket in its red wax coating, is a somewhat mild cheese that makes an equally mild fondue. But more and more stores are also stocking aged Gouda, which is drier and sharper and will crank up the flavor a few notches. The Dutch cooks add a shot of gin to their fondue, but I prefer the softer spiciness of caraway seeds.

What to Dip

Rye or mixed-grain bread, cut into bite-sized cubes (leave a piece of crust on each cube) • Smoked ham, cut into bite-sized cubes • Cooked smoked sausage, such as kielbasa, cut into wedges • Sour gherkins (cornichons)

1 garlic clove, peeled

1 cup Danish beer, such as Heineken

1 tablespoon fresh lemon juice

12 ounces Gouda cheese, rind removed, cut into small cubes (about 3½ cups)

4 ounces aged Gouda, shredded (1½ cups)

5 teaspoons cornstarch

1 tablespoon gin, or 1½ teaspoons caraway seeds, coarsely crushed in a mortar or under a heavy saucepan

Freshly ground pepper, to taste

1. Rub the inside of a medium, heavy-bottomed saucepan with the garlic; discard the garlic. Add the beer and lemon juice and bring to a simmer over medium heat.

2. In a medium bowl, toss the cheeses with the cornstarch. Gradually stir the cheeses into the saucepan, stirring until the first addition is melted before adding another. Stir in the gin or the caraway seeds. Season with the pepper.

3. Transfer the fondue to a cheese fondue pot and keep warm over a fondue burner. Serve immediately, with dipping ingredients of your choice.

French Gruyère and Onion Fondue

ARE YOU ONE of those people (like me) whose favorite part of a bowl of French onion soup is the melted cheese on top? In this luscious fondue, we get to indulge in this passion. It's difficult for me to choose my favorite fondue, but if pressed, this would be the winner.

What to Dip

Crusty French or Italian bread, cut into cubes (leave a piece of crust on each cube) • Roast beef tenderloin, cut into cubes • Tart, crisp apples, cut into slices, tossed with lemon juice to discourage browning

2 tablespoons unsalted butter

1 large onion, finely chopped

½ cup dry white wine

½ cup beef stock, preferably homemade, or reduced-sodium beef stock

1 tablespoon white wine vinegar

1 pound Gruyère cheese, rind trimmed and discarded, shredded (6 cups)

2 tablespoons all-purpose flour

1 tablespoon Cognac or brandy

1½ teaspoons finely chopped fresh thyme or ½ teaspoon dried thyme

Freshly ground pepper, to taste

1. In a medium, heavy-bottomed saucepan, melt the butter over medium heat. Add the onion and cook, stirring often, until the onion is dark golden brown, about 10 minutes. Add the wine, stock, and vinegar and bring to a simmer.

2. In a medium bowl, toss the cheese with the flour. A handful at a time, stir the cheese into the saucepan, stirring the first addition until melted before adding the next. Allow the fondue to bubble lightly a few times, but do not bring to a boil. Stir in the Cognac and thyme. Season with the pepper.

3. Transfer the fondue to a cheese fondue pot and keep warm over a fondue burner. Serve immediately, with dipping ingredients of your choice.

Greek Kasseri Fondue

makes 4 to 6 servings

HAVE YOU EVER been to a Greek restaurant and seen a waiter running by with a flaming dish held over his head? It's probably that famous Greek appetizer, fried Kasseri cheese flamed with brandy or ouzo. The fondue version is less nerve-racking, and just as tasty.

What to Dip

Pita bread, split and toasted, cut into wedges • Raw zucchini, cut into wedges • Cherry tomatoes • Small mushroom caps

1 garlic clove, peeled

1¼ cups dry white wine

1 tablespoon fresh lemon juice

1 pound Kasseri cheese, thick rind trimmed and
    discarded, shredded (about 4 cups)

1 tablespoon cornstarch

2 tablespoons brandy, preferably Greek Metaxa

1½ tablespoons chopped fresh dill (optional)

Freshly ground pepper, to taste

1. Rub the inside of a medium, heavy-bottomed saucepan with the garlic; discard the garlic. Add the wine and lemon juice and bring to a simmer over medium heat.

2. In a medium bowl, toss the cheese with the cornstarch. Gradually stir the cheese into the saucepan, allowing the previous addition to melt before adding another. Let the fondue bubble briefly, but do not allow to come to a boil. Stir in the brandy, and the dill, if using. Season with the pepper.

3. Transfer the fondue to a cheese fondue pot and keep warm over a fondue burner. Serve immediately, with dipping ingredients of your choice.

Spanish Manchego and Green Olive Fondue

makes 4 to 6 servings

T HIS SPANISH-INSPIRED FONDUE is milk based and finished with a dose of dry sherry. It needs a bit of lemon juice to balance the flavors, but add it at the end—if added earlier, it could curdle the milk.

What to Dip

Crusty French or Italian bread, cut into bite-sized cubes (leave a piece of crust on each cube) • Cooked smoked (hard) chorizo sausage, cut into rounds • Raw red bell pepper slices

1 garlic clove, peeled

1¼ cups milk

1 pound Manchego cheese, rind removed, cut into small cubes (about 5 cups)

1 tablespoon cornstarch

½ cup finely chopped pimento-stuffed olives

2 tablespoons dry sherry

¼ teaspoon crushed hot red pepper flakes

2 tablespoons fresh lemon juice

Sweet paprika, for garnish

1 Rub the inside of a medium, heavy-bottomed saucepan with the garlic; discard the garlic. Add the milk and bring to a simmer over medium heat.

2 In a medium bowl, toss the cheese with the cornstarch. Stir the cheese into the saucepan, a handful at a time, stirring the first addition until melted before adding the next. Allow the fondue to bubble lightly a few times, but do not bring to a boil. Stir in the olives, sherry, red pepper flakes, and lemon juice.

continued

3. Transfer the fondue to a cheese fondue pot and keep warm over a fondue burner. Sprinkle with a dusting of paprika. Serve immediately, with dipping ingredients of your choice.

California Artichoke, Red Pepper, and Monterey Jack Fondue

makes 6 to 8 servings

MONTEREY JACK IS a great fondue cheese, melting into a smooth, thick creaminess. This fondue is chunky with the flavors of northern California—artichokes, garlic, red peppers, and of course, wine. It makes a big batch for a large group of friends.

2 tablespoons extra-virgin
    olive oil

1 medium onion, finely chopped

1 medium red bell pepper,
    seeded and finely chopped

2 garlic cloves, minced

1 (10-ounce) package thawed
    artichoke hearts, finely
    chopped

What to Dip

Crusty sourdough bread, cut into bite-sized cubes (leave a piece of crust on each cube) • Cooked shrimp, peeled and deveined • Cooked chicken breast, skinned and boned, cut into bite-sized cubes • Asparagus spears, prepared for dipping (see page 14) • Raw celery sticks • Raw fennel bulb, cut into sticks • Small mushroom caps • Boiled new potatoes

1 tablespoon finely chopped fresh rosemary or
   1 teaspoon crumbled dried rosemary
1 teaspoon finely chopped fresh thyme or ½ teaspoon
   dried thyme
1 cup dry white wine
1 tablespoon fresh lemon juice
1 pound Monterey Jack cheese, shredded (5 cups)
2 ounces freshly grated Parmigiano-Reggiano cheese
   (½ cup)
1 tablespoon cornstarch
Freshly ground pepper, to taste

1. In a large skillet over medium heat, heat the oil. Add the onion, red pepper, and garlic. Cook, stirring occasionally, until the onion is golden, about 5 minutes. Stir in the artichoke hearts, rosemary, and thyme. Cook, stirring often, until heated through, about 2 minutes.

2. Transfer the artichoke mixture to a medium, heavy-bottomed saucepan. Add the wine and lemon juice and bring to a simmer over medium heat.

3 In a medium bowl, toss the cheeses with the cornstarch. Gradually stir the cheese mixture into the saucepan, stirring until the first addition is melted before adding another. Season with the pepper.

4. Transfer the fondue to a ceramic or enameled cast-iron fondue pot and keep warm over a fondue burner. Serve immediately, with dipping ingredients of your choice.

Mexican Fondue with Chorizo

makes 4 to 6 servings

Here's a *CHILE con queso* for purists, one that eschews weird orange "cheese product" and uses a blend of Jack and Cheddar to make the best version this side of the border. In some areas, there are two kinds of chorizo—a soft bulk sausage and hard smoked links. This uses the hard links.

What to Dip

Tortilla chips • Cooked shrimp • Cooked chicken breast, skinned and boned, cut into cubes • Marinated artichoke hearts • Broccoli or cauliflower florets, prepared for dipping (see page 14) • Raw red bell pepper strips • Raw zucchini rounds

1 tablespoon olive oil

6 ounces hard chorizo sausage, casings removed, finely chopped

1 medium red onion, finely chopped

1 jalapeño pepper, seeded and minced

1 garlic clove, crushed through a press

2 teaspoons chili powder

1 teaspoon dried oregano

½ teaspoon ground cumin

1 (16-ounce) can tomatoes in juice, drained and finely chopped

1 cup lager beer

½ pound extra-sharp Cheddar cheese, shredded (about 3 cups)

½ pound Monterey Jack cheese, shredded (about 3 cups)

1 tablespoon cornstarch

Hot red pepper sauce, preferably Mexican, to taste

Chopped fresh cilantro, for garnish

1. In a medium, heavy-bottomed saucepan, heat the oil over medium heat. Add the chorizo and cook, stirring often, until the chorizo is lightly browned and releases some fat, about 5 minutes. Pour off all but 1 tablespoon of the fat. Add the onion, jalapeño pepper, and garlic and cover. Cook, stirring occasionally, until the onion is softened, about 4 minutes. Add the chili powder, oregano, and cumin and stir for 30 seconds. Add the tomatoes and cook until their juices evaporate and the mixture is somewhat dry, about 3 minutes. Add the beer and bring to a simmer.

2. In a medium bowl, toss the cheeses with the cornstarch. A handful at a time, stir the cheeses into the saucepan, stirring until the first addition is melted before adding another. Add red pepper sauce, to taste.

3. Transfer to a cheese fondue pot and keep warm over a fondue burner. Sprinkle with the cilantro. Serve immediately, with the dipping ingredients of your choice.

Sun-Dried Tomato Pizza Fondue

makes 6 to 8 servings

PIZZA IS RIGHT up there with fondue as one of America's most fun-to-eat and delicious foods, so a pizza-flavored fondue seems in order. Focaccia, the Italian flatbread, is the perfect dipping ingredient, as it resembles a topping-less pizza crust.

2 tablespoons extra-virgin olive oil

1 medium onion, chopped

½ cup finely chopped sun-dried tomatoes (not oil-packed) or sun-dried tomato salad bits

1 garlic clove, minced

½ teaspoon dried oregano

½ teaspoon dried basil

¼ teaspoon crushed hot red pepper flakes

1 cup dry white wine

12 ounces mozzarella cheese, shredded (about 3 cups)

4 ounces sharp Provolone cheese, shredded (about 1½ cups)

2 ounces freshly grated Parmigiano-Reggiano cheese (½ cup)

1 tablespoon cornstarch

What to Dip

Crusty French or Italian bread, cut into bite-sized cubes (leave a piece of crust on each cube) • Focaccia, cut into bite-sized squares • Italian salami, cut into bite-sized cubes • Pepperoni, cut into wedges • Cooked baby artichoke hearts • Broccoli florets, prepared for dipping (see page 14) • Raw red bell pepper slices • Raw zucchini, cut into wedges

1. In a medium, heavy-bottomed saucepan, heat the oil over medium heat. Add the onion and cook, stirring often, until translucent, about 4 minutes. Add the sun-dried tomatoes, garlic, oregano, basil, and hot pepper flakes. Stir until the garlic is fragrant, about 1 minute. Add the wine and bring to a simmer.

2. In a medium bowl, toss the cheeses with the cornstarch. Stir the cheeses, a handful at a time, into the saucepan, stirring until the first addition is melted before adding another. Let the fondue come to a bare simmer, but do not boil.

3. Transfer to cheese fondue pot and keep warm over a fondue burner. Serve immediately, with the dipping ingredients of your choice.

Pizza Fondue with Olives: Stir ½ cup finely chopped pitted black Mediterranean olives into the fondue.

Hot Crab Fondue Outré

EVERY COOK HAS recipes on file that they consider "secret weapons," recipes that transcend trends and never go out of style. Hot crab fondue is hardly a new wave recipe, but the mention that it will be on my menu guarantees that the people on the guest list will RSVP with their acceptances faster than usual. (I have to admit that it's so wonderfully rich it may work better as a party dip with bread cubes and crudités than as a main course fondue.) It uses Old Bay seasoning, a multi-spice blend from the Chesapeake Bay region that is especially complementary to seafood.

What to Dip

Toasted French bread rounds • Breadsticks • Tortilla chips • Cooked shrimp, peeled and deveined • Broccoli florets, prepared for dipping (see page 14)

1 tablespoon unsalted butter

2 tablespoons minced shallots or white parts of scallions

3 tablespoons dry vermouth or white wine

1 cup half-and-half or light cream

8 ounces cream cheese, cut into small cubes, at room temperature

4 ounces Cheddar cheese, shredded (about 1¼ cups)

½ pound crabmeat, flaked and picked over for cartilage

2 tablespoons lemon juice

2 teaspoons Dijon mustard

1 teaspoon Worcestershire sauce

½ teaspoon Old Bay seasoning

Hot pepper sauce, to taste

Chopped fresh parsley or chives, for garnish

1. In a medium, heavy-bottomed saucepan, melt the butter over medium heat. Add the shallots and cook, stirring often, until softened, about 2 minutes. Add the vermouth and bring to a boil. Add the half-and-half and bring to a simmer.

2. Gradually whisk in the cream cheese, whisking until the first addition is smooth and melted before adding another. Stir in the Cheddar cheese until melted. Stir in the crab, lemon juice, mustard, Worcestershire sauce, and Old Bay seasoning. Season with the hot sauce.

3. Transfer to an earthenware or enameled cast-iron fondue pot and keep warm over a fondue burner. Sprinkle with the parsley. Serve immediately, with the dipping ingredients of your choice.

Lobster Newburg Fondue

makes 4 to 6 servings

IT WAS MY friend Claudia McQuillan, in her book, *Chips and Dips*, who reminded me of the long-ago pleasures of lobster Newburg—a creamy, sherry-spiked dish that used to be everywhere, but now is found only in *outré* restaurants. Claudia, too, makes a lobster Newburg dip, and while my recipe is different, I thank her for both the inspiration and the memories.

2 tablespoons unsalted butter

2 tablespoons finely chopped shallots or white parts of
    scallions

3 tablespoons all-purpose flour

½ cup dry white wine

2 tablespoons dry sherry, such
    as Manzanillo

½ cup chicken stock, preferably
    homemade, or reduced-
    sodium canned broth

½ cup heavy cream

1 pound Gruyère cheese, rind trimmed and discarded,
    and shredded (about 5 cups)

8 ounces (1½ cups) chopped cooked lobster meat
    (see Note)

1 tablespoon finely chopped fresh parsley

⅛ teaspoon salt

Freshly ground pepper, to taste

What to Dip

Crusty French bread, cut into cubes • Cooked shrimp, peeled and deveined • Cooked baby artichoke hearts • Parboiled asparagus spears • Small mushroom caps

1. In a medium, heavy-bottomed saucepan, melt the butter over medium heat. Add the shallots and cook, stirring often, until softened, about 2 minutes. Whisk in the flour and reduce the heat to low. Stir and cook, without browning the flour, for 1 minute. Whisk in the wine and sherry, then the chicken stock and heavy cream.

2. Increase the heat to high and bring to a simmer. Reduce the heat to low and simmer for 5 minutes. Gradually stir in the cheese, stirring each addition until it is melted. Stir in the lobster and parsley. Season with the salt and pepper.

3. Transfer to a cheese fondue pot and keep warm over a fondue burner. Serve immediately, with the dipping ingredients of your choice.

Note: Some fish stores sell fresh lobster meat in containers, but avoid canned lobster meat. A new convenience is supermarket fish counters that take a whole live lobster from their tanks and cook it for you. The tail and claw meat from a 1¼-pound lobster will give you the 1½ cups needed for this recipe.

Normandy Shrimp Fondue with Cider and Gruyère

makes 4 to 6 servings

T HROUGHOUT THE WORLD, the best cooking is done with what is on hand. For example, Normandy, a French province, is noted for its apples and seafood. Therefore, you'll find seafood dishes cooked with hard cider, not wine, and they are delicious.

> **What to Dip**
>
> Crusty French or Italian bread, cut into bite-sized cubes (leave a piece of crust on each cube) • Broccoli florets, prepared for dipping (see page 14) • Small mushroom caps

3 tablespoons unsalted butter

1 pound medium shrimp,

    peeled, deveined, and

    coarsely chopped

4 ounces fresh mushrooms, finely chopped (1⅓ cups)

2 tablespoons finely chopped shallots

1 cup hard cider or ½ cup nonalcoholic apple cider and

    ½ cup dry white wine

1 tablespoon fresh lemon juice

1 pound rindless Gruyère cheese, shredded

    (about 5 cups)

1 tablespoon cornstarch

2 teaspoons finely chopped fresh tarragon or

    1 teaspoon dried tarragon

Freshly ground pepper, to taste

1. In a medium, heavy-bottomed saucepan, melt 1½ table-spoons of the butter over medium-high heat. Add the shrimp

and cook, stirring often, until they turn pink and firm, about 2 minutes. Transfer to a bowl and set aside.

2. Add the remaining 1½ tablespoons butter to the saucepan and melt. Add the mushrooms and cook, stirring often, until they give off their juices, it evaporates, and the mushrooms begin to brown, about 5 minutes. Add the shallots and cook until softened, about 1 minute. Add the cider and lemon juice and bring to a simmer.

3. In a medium bowl, toss the cheese with the cornstarch. A handful at a time, stir the cheese into the saucepan, stirring until the first addition is melted before adding another. Stir in the tarragon, and season with the pepper.

4. Transfer to a cheese fondue pot and keep warm over a fondue burner. Serve immediately, with the dipping ingredients of your choice.

Smoked Salmon, Capers, and Triple-Crème Fondue

makes 4 to 6 servings

FONDUE—IT'S JUST not for dinner anymore. Here's another fondue that I keep in mind when I have friends coming by for a weekend brunch. It comes together in nothing flat, leaving plenty of time for cooks to enjoy their guests. I like to make the fondue with Champagne, which is certainly most people's first choice as a brunch beverage, and serve it with plenty of bubbly, too.

continued

¾ cup dry Champagne or white
wine (sparkling or still)

1 tablespoon fresh lemon juice

1 pound triple-crème cheese,
such as Explorateur, well
chilled, rind trimmed and
discarded, cut into small
cubes (about 2½ cups)

1 tablespoon cornstarch

8 ounces smoked salmon, finely chopped

2 tablespoons rinsed bottled capers (coarsely chopped,
if not small nonpareil)

1 tablespoon finely chopped fresh chives or dill

Freshly ground white pepper, to taste

What to Dip

Toasted English muffins,
cut into wedges • Cooked
shrimp, peeled and
deveined • Asparagus
spears, prepared for
dipping (see page 14) •
Cherry tomatoes

1. In a medium, heavy-bottomed saucepan, heat the Champagne and lemon juice until barely simmering over medium heat.

2. In a medium bowl, mash and stir the cheese with the cornstarch until combined. Gradually stir the cheese into the saucepan, stirring until the first addition is melted before adding another. Stir in the salmon, capers, and chives. Season with the pepper.

3. Transfer to a cheese fondue pot and keep warm over a fondue burner. Serve immediately, with the dipping ingredients of your choice.

Fearless
Fried Fondue

*I*MAGINE we're grape pickers in Burgundy, rushing to pick the harvest before it gets too ripe. It's an intensely busy period, with not a moment to spare for a meal. No time to eat? That's an affront to the entire French way of life! French ingenuity comes to the rescue. A small fire of grape vines is built in a clearing, and a pot of grapeseed oil is put on to heat. We cut up meat into small pieces that will fry quickly, spear them on our knives, and dip the cubes into the oil to cook . . . *voilà!* Dinner is served.

That's one legend behind how fondue Bourguignonne (Burgundian fondue) was born. But the truth may be less romantic. Sometime after World War II, Swiss cooks began cooking meat in hot oil as an alternative to their beloved cheese fondue—a kind of French-fried meat supper. It became known as fondue Bourguignonne because the French-speaking Swiss are descended from the Burgundians. The first written reference to hot oil fondue seems to have been in a Swiss women's magazine about forty years ago. Of course, deep-fried foods have a long history, from tempura to fried calamari. What makes fondue Bourguignonne different is that the food is not dipped in a batter. It is entirely impractical to expect guests to dip food into batter at the table and then fry it themselves in a communal pot. The batter drips all over the tablecloth, bits of cooked batter break off and burn in the oil, and it is hard to drain the cooked food well. In other words, keep it simple. Cook the meat, poultry, or seafood *au naturel*, with complementary sauces, a big green salad, and lots of crusty bread.

This chapter also has a fondue that isn't made with cheese, chocolate, or broth—*bagna cauda*. It didn't fit into easy categorization, but with olive oil is its main ingredient, I thought it would feel comfortable in this company.

Equipment

Never make fondue Bouguignonne in a ceramic cheese fondue pot! The hot oil will break the pot. More than one dinner party (not to mention the dining room table) has been ruined this way. Fondue sets often come with either very sketchy instructions translated from another language, or no instructions at all, and they very often leave out this imperative piece of information.

A fondue Bourguignonne pot is metal, with short handles. (A long handle that sticks out could get knocked over.) The pot should sit firmly on its burner and not rock at all. The burner unit should have a strong enough flame to keep the oil temperature at 360° to 375°F.—alcohol burners are best. As with all fondue pots, be sure to protect the table by placing the burner on a trivet. Electric fondue pots are one of the best choices for fondue Bouguignonne fans, but connect the pot to a very long extension cord that can be safely plugged in without anyone tripping over it.

Another important feature of a good fondue Bourguignonne pot is its shape, which should be curved in at the top to shield oil splatters. Some pots have notches at the top for holding the forks of cooking meat in the oil so they don't have to be held by the guests. A regular saucepan (preferably with short, curved handles on both sides) can substitute for a true fondue pot, but the curved top with fork notches makes the real pot uniquely practical for this kind of cooking.

Long metal fondue forks are a must for fondue Bourguignonne. However, they get hot in the oil, so warn your guests that it is not a good idea to eat their cooked food directly from their fork. To make eating easier, provide a plate for them to put the food on and a dinner fork for eating.

A deep-frying thermometer is an essential tool for telling when the oil has reached the frying temperature on the stove, and can remain in the pot to check the temperature throughout the meal.

Ingredients

In deep-frying, the decisions begin with choosing the cooking fat. I prefer vegetable shortening, which has less odor than other fats or oils. Vegetable shortening is more highly refined than vegetable oil, so it has fewer components that give off that "deep-fried" smell. Of course, vegetable oil will work, too.

Grapeseed oil and peanut oil are often touted as being the perfect deep-frying oils because of their high smoking points (the temperature at which heated oil starts to smoke and its flavor deteriorates) and mild flavor. But they are prohibitively expensive, unless you can get them in bulk at a restaurant supply store. Olive oil is a fine choice, and, contrary to popular opinion, will not begin to smoke any sooner than other fats as long as it is kept below its smoke point of 390°F. In fact, Italian cooks not only deep-fry with olive oil, but the best cooks use only extra-virgin! Olive oil is much less expensive in Italy.

Some cooks strain deep-frying fat through a wire sieve and store it in the refrigerator for another use. Frankly, I use deep-frying fat once, and factor its minor cost into the meal's budget. My refrigerator and freezer are full of things I am swearing to use one day, only to be useless by the time I get around to them.

All meat, poultry, and seafood should be cut into bite-sized cubes. Allow 6 to 8 ounces of boneless meat per person. There is no need to cut it into the paper-thin slices used for Asian hot pots. Pick lean, tender cuts of meat that will cook quickly—for example, beef tenderloin, not beef chuck. The food should be removed from the refrigerator 30 minutes before cooking. Chilled food will make the oil splatter. Again, *au naturel* is the name of the game. It may be tempting to marinate the meat or rub it with spices or herbs. However, the wet marinade tends to cause splattering, and the dried herbs fall off the meat and burn in the oil.

Part of the fun of serving fondue Bourguignonne is offering an assortment of sauces with the meat—at least two, or even four. Each recipe features a single meat with one complementary sauce to give an idea of the basic procedure, and suggests other sauces, too. While the sauces can and should be prepared well ahead of time, if they have been refrigerated, let them come to room temperature. Never serve ice-cold sauces. Many fondue cooks make classic, French roux or hollandaise-based sauces for their meals. This doesn't make any sense to me, as these sauces are best served hot (or at least warm), and it is hard to keep them at their proper temperature throughout the meal. I much prefer making sauces that are delicious at room temperature. Most of these sauces can be made in minutes.

Making and Serving Fondue Bourguignonne

The cooking oil should be heated in the metal fondue pot on top of the kitchen stove. Tabletop burners are not strong enough to raise the oil to 375°F., the optimum temperature for frying the meat, although it can be cooked properly down to 360°F. To allow for the oil bubbling when the meat is added, never fill a meat fondue pot more than half full. Transfer the pot to the fondue burner with the flame adjusted to high. To reduce the amount of deep-frying odor in the house, open a window or turn on the air conditioning to encourage ventilation. Many of my Swiss friends serve fondue Bourguignonne outside on a terrace or screened porch to circumvent the problem entirely.

Each place setting should have a dinner plate; a fondue fork for cooking the meat; another fork for eating the meat from the plate (those fondue forks get hot in that oil!); and a folded paper towel on a saucer to blot oil off the meat. If one platter of meat doesn't seem to be enough for all of the diners to reach it without straining, simply make two smaller platters. Don't forget to remove the meat from the refrigerator at least 30 minutes before serving to take off the chill. Offer bowls of the sauces, each with its own serving spoon for dolloping sauce onto the plates.

The diners cook one cube of meat at a time, blot it on their paper towel, transfer it to their plate and dip it into one of the sauces to eat with their dinner fork. The oil temperature will drop when the meat is added, and the more forks in the pot, the more quickly the temperature reduces. Try to get the guests to stagger their cooking with no more than three forks in the pot at a time. If the temperature drops below 360°F. (keep the deep-frying thermometer attached to the pot as a gauge), stop cooking and let the oil temperature rise before adding more food. Low temperatures allow the food to soak up the oil, whereas hot temperatures seal the outside of the food and keep the oil out. Actually, it is easy to tell if the temperature is right: when the food is added, the oil will bubble around it immediately. It is hard to give an exact cooking time for the meat, as there are so many variables that affect the exact cooking temperature. Each guest needs to experiment to discover how long it takes for the meat to cook to his or her preferred doneness. Again—it's all in the fun.

Don't forget to serve a hearty salad. Not only does it fill out the meal, but while the guests are nibbling their greens, instead of cooking their meat, the oil gets the time it needs to come back up to temperature.

Classic Beef Fondue with Sour Cream and Horseradish Sauce

makes 4 to 6 servings

BEEF FONDUE IS the true fondue Bourguignonne, and our point of departure for all other fried fondues. Beef tenderloin is the best choice, but be sure to trim it well of all fat and membrane.

Sour Cream and Horseradish Sauce

¾ cup sour cream

2 tablespoons prepared horseradish

1 whole scallion, white and green parts, finely chopped

1 teaspoon fresh lemon juice

¼ teaspoon salt

⅛ teaspoon freshly ground pepper

Vegetable shortening, for deep-frying

2 pounds beef tenderloin, well trimmed, cut into ¾-inch cubes

Other Sauces

Aioli (page 83) •
Roquefort Mayonnaise (page 84)

1. To make the horseradish sauce, combine the sour cream, horseradish, scallion, lemon juice, salt, and pepper in a small bowl. Cover and let stand at room temperature for 1 hour for the flavors to blend. (The sauce can be prepared up to 1 day ahead, covered and refrigerated. Serve at room temperature.) Makes about 1 cup.

continued

2. Melt enough vegetable shortening in a metal fondue pot to come halfway up the sides. Heat on the kitchen stove over high heat until a deep-frying thermometer reads 375°F. Transfer the pot to a fondue burner with a high flame.

3. Allow guests to cook their meat to their own taste. Serve with the horseradish sauce, along with any additional sauces.

Lamb Fondue with Balsamic Vinegar-Mint Sauce

makes 4 to 6 servings

BONELESS LEG OF lamb makes a terrific fondue. As with all fondue meats, be sure all excess fat is trimmed away. The sauce is simplicity itself. Serve it in individual ramekins so it doesn't run all over the plate. Fresh mint is a must.

Balsamic Vinegar-Mint Sauce

¼ cup water

1 tablespoon light brown sugar

1 garlic clove, crushed through
    a press

½ cup balsamic vinegar

⅓ cup chopped fresh mint

Vegetable shortening, for deep-frying

2 pounds boneless leg of lamb, well trimmed, cut into
    ¾-inch cubes

Other Sauces

Aioli (page 83) • Aioli with Anchovy and Rosemary (page 83) • Greek Yogurt and Cucumber Sauce (page 88) • Roasted Red Pepper and Almond Sauce (page 90)

1. To make the mint sauce, bring the water, brown sugar, and garlic to a simmer over medium heat, stirring to dissolve the sugar. Add the balsamic vinegar and bring just to a simmer. Stir in the mint. Remove from the heat and let stand at room temperature for at least 2 hours for the flavors to blend. (The sauce can be prepared up to 8 hours ahead, kept at room temperature.) Makes about ¾ cup.

2. Melt enough vegetable shortening in a metal fondue pot to come halfway up the sides. Heat on the kitchen stove over high heat until a deep-frying thermometer reads 375°F. Transfer the pot to a fondue burner with a high flame.

3. Allow guests to cook their meat to their own taste. Serve with the mint sauce, along with any additional sauces.

Pork Fondue with Southwestern Chipotle Mayonnaise

makes 4 to 6 servings

MAKE THIS FONDUE with pork tenderloin or a center cut of pork loin. When choosing sauces, sometimes I like to give the selection a Southwestern feel: the guacamole, chipotle, and BBQ-flavored sauces all go well with the pork. Don't overcook the pork, or it will be tough.

Other Sauces

Asian Orange Sauce (page 74) • Easy Peanut Sauce (page 87) • Ginger Dipping Sauce (page 86, served in individual ramekins) • Guacamole Mayonnaise (page 84) • Quick BBQ Sauce (page 92)

Southwestern Chipotle Mayonnaise

1 cup Aioli (page 83)

2 minced canned chipotle peppers *en adobo*

1 teaspoon sauce (*adobo*) from the peppers

1 garlic clove, crushed through a press

½ teaspoon ground cumin

½ teaspoon dried oregano

Vegetable shortening, for deep-frying

2 pounds pork tenderloin or boneless pork loin, cut into ¾-inch cubes

1. To make the chipotle mayonnaise, combine the aioli, minced chipotle peppers, their adobo, the garlic, cumin, and oregano in a small bowl. Cover and let stand at room temperature for 1 hour to allow the flavors to blend. (The sauce can be prepared up to 1 day ahead, covered and refrigerated. Serve at room temperature.) Makes about 1 cup.

2. Melt enough vegetable shortening in a metal fondue pot to come halfway up the sides. Heat on the kitchen stove over high heat until a deep-frying thermometer reads 375°F. Transfer the pot to a fondue burner with a high flame.

3. Allow guests to cook their meat to their own taste, keeping in mind that the pork should be lightly browned, but not over-cooked. Serve with the chipotle mayonnaise, along with any additional sauces.

German Sausage Fondue
with Apple Butter Mustard

makes 4 to 6 servings

THIS INDULGENT FONDUE makes me nostalgic for the annual Oktoberfest parties my relatives from Liechtenstein threw when I was growing up—ah, I can hear the polkas now. The culinary highlight was platters piled high with fried sausages. Serve the fondue with a few different kinds of sausages and a selection of mustard-based sauces, completing the meal German-style with a bowl of potato salad.

Other Sauces

Hot and Sweet Mustard
(page 89) • Quick BBQ
Sauce (page 92)

Apple Butter Mustard

⅓ cup high-quality apple butter
   (made from only apples and cider)

⅓ cup Dijon mustard

Vegetable shortening, for deep-frying

2 pounds assorted sausages, such as knockwurst,
   bockwurst, bratwurst, and kielbasa, cut into
   wedges about ½ inch thick

1. To make the apple butter mustard, combine the apple butter and mustard in a small bowl. Cover and let stand at room temperature for at least 1 hour for the flavors to blend. (The mustard can be prepared up to 3 days ahead, covered and refrigerated. Serve at room temperature.) Makes ⅔ cup.

2. Melt enough vegetable shortening in a metal fondue pot to come halfway up the sides. Heat on the kitchen stove over high

heat until a deep-frying thermometer reads 375°F. Transfer the pot to a fondue burner with a high flame.

3. Allow guests to cook their sausages until browned around the edges. Serve with the apple butter mustard, along with any additional sauces.

Chicken Fondue with Quick Béarnaise Sauce

makes 4 to 6 servings

EVERYONE LIKES FRIED chicken; cooked the fondue way, the chicken flavor really comes through. Boneless, skinless chicken breast works best, as dark meat takes a little too long to cook through for my patience. There are so many sauces that would work here, it's difficult to decide beyond the mock béarnaise. Traditional béarnaise is derived from hollandaise, and should be served warm—something that is not too easy to pull off during a leisurely fondue meal—and this easier version is hardly a compromise.

Other Sauces

Apple Butter Mustard (page 68) • Easy Peanut Sauce (page 87) • Greek Yogurt and Cucumber Sauce (page 88) • Pesto Mayonnaise (page 84) • Roasted Red Pepper and Almond Sauce (page 90) • Southwestern Chipotle Mayonnaise (page 66) • Quick BBQ Sauce (page 92)

Quick Béarnaise Sauce

½ cup Homemade Mayonnaise
    (page 82), or store-bought
1 tablespoon minced shallots
2 teaspoons chopped fresh
    tarragon or 1 teaspoon
    dried tarragon
1 teaspoon tarragon or red wine vinegar
⅛ teaspoon freshly ground white pepper

Vegetable shortening, for deep-frying
2 pounds boneless, skinless chicken breast, cut into
    ¾-inch cubes

1. To make the quick béarnaise, combine the mayonnaise, shallots, tarragon, vinegar, and pepper in a small bowl. Cover and let stand at room temperature to blend the flavors, at least 1 hour. (The dip can be prepared up to 1 day ahead, covered and refrigerated. Remove from the refrigerator 1 hour before serving.) Makes about ⅔ cup.

2. Melt enough vegetable shortening in a metal fondue pot to come halfway up the sides. Heat on the kitchen stove over high heat until a deep-frying thermometer reads 375°F. Transfer the pot to a fondue burner with a high flame.

3. Allow guests to cook their chicken until browned around the edges and cooked through without becoming dried out or tough. Serve with the quick béarnaise sauce, along with any additional sauces.

Turkey Fondue with Cranberry-Lime Mayonnaise

makes 4 to 6 servings

TURKEY AND CRANBERRIES are an American institution—the Fred and Ginger of the food world. Boneless, skinless turkey breast or breast tenderloins are easy to cut into bite-sized cubes, or cut turkey breast cutlets into ¾-inch squares.

> **Other Sauces**
>
> **Apple Butter Mustard (page 68)** • **Asian Orange Sauce (page 74)**

Cranberry-Lime Mayonnaise

½ cup jellied cranberry sauce

2 tablespoons lime juice

½ cup Homemade Mayonnaise (page 82) or store-bought

Grated zest of 1 lime

Vegetable shortening, for deep-frying

2 pounds boneless, skinless turkey breast, cut into
   ¾-inch cubes

1. To make the cranberry mayonnaise, mash the cranberry sauce and lime juice together in a small bowl with a rubber spatula until well mixed and the cranberry sauce is smooth. Stir in the mayonnaise and lime zest. Cover and let stand at room temperature for at least 1 hour for the flavors to blend. (The mayonnaise can be prepared up to 3 days ahead, covered and refrigerated. Serve at room temperature.) Makes about 1 cup.

2. Melt enough vegetable shortening in a metal fondue pot to come halfway up the sides. Heat on the kitchen stove over high heat until a deep-frying thermometer reads 375°F. Transfer the pot to a fondue burner with a high flame.

3. Allow guests to cook their turkey until browned around the edges and cooked through without becoming dried out or tough. Serve with the cranberry mayonnaise, along with any additional sauces.

Duck Fondue with Asian Orange Sauce

makes 4 to 6 servings

D UCK BREAST, WITH its beeflike texture and flavor, makes a sophisticated fondue for special occasions. Large boneless Moulard duck breasts (sometimes called *magrets*), are available at many specialty food stores and fine butchers. Supermarkets usually carry whole Pekin (Long Island) ducks—ask the butcher to bone out the breasts, save the legs for a stew, make the carcass into a soup, and render the fat and skin for cooking. Skinless, boneless Moulard breasts weigh about 11 ounces each, Pekin only about 7 ounces. Any way you cut it, duck breasts are pricy; you may want to make them a part of a "mixed grill" fondue, combined with beef and chicken.

Other Sauces

Apple Butter Mustard (page 68) • Cranberry-Lime Mayonnaise (page 72) • Ginger Dipping Sauce (page 86)

Asian Orange Sauce

2 tablespoons dry mustard

2 tablespoons water

½ cup hoisin sauce

¼ cup fresh orange juice

Grated zest of 1 orange

Vegetable shortening, for deep-frying

2 pounds boneless, skinless duck breast, cut into ¾-inch cubes

1. To make the orange sauce, in a small bowl, mix the mustard and water into a paste. Stir in the hoisin sauce, orange juice,

and zest. Cover and let stand at room temperature for at least 1 hour for the flavors to blend. (The sauce can be prepared up to 1 day ahead, covered and refrigerated. Serve at room temperature.) Makes about 1 cup.

2. Melt enough vegetable shortening in a metal fondue pot to come halfway up the sides. Heat on the kitchen stove over high heat until a deep-frying thermometer reads 375°F. Transfer the pot to a fondue burner with a high flame.

3. Allow guests to cook their duck just until browned around the edges—duck breast is best served medium-rare. Serve with the orange sauce, along with any additional sauces.

Swordfish Fondue with Tapenade Mayonnaise

makes 4 to 6 servings

OF ALL FISH, swordfish is the best candidate for fondue owing to its firm flesh—a fondue fork just won't stay speared into many other fishes. Tapenade mayonnaise is a perfect match.

Other Sauces

Aioli with Anchovy and Rosemary (page 83) •
Greek Yogurt and Cucumber Sauce (page 88) •
Pesto Mayonnaise (page 84)
• Remoulade Sauce (page 83) • Tartar Sauce (page 78)

Tapenade Mayonnaise

½ cup pitted black Mediterranean olives

2 tablespoons bottled capers, rinsed

1 tablespoon Dijon mustard

3 anchovy fillets in oil, drained and chopped, or
1 teaspoon anchovy paste

1 teaspoon fresh lemon juice

1 teaspoon Cognac or brandy

1 garlic clove, crushed through a press

¼ teaspoon crushed hot red pepper flakes

½ cup Homemade Mayonnaise (page 82), or store-bought

Vegetable shortening, for deep-frying

2 pounds (¼-inch-thick) swordfish steaks, cut into ¾-inch cubes

1. To make the tapenade mayonnaise, combine the olives, capers, mustard, anchovies, lemon juice, Cognac, garlic, and

red pepper flakes in a food processor fitted with the metal blade. Pulse until the mixture becomes a coarse paste. Transfer to a small bowl and stir in the mayonnaise. Cover and let stand at room temperature for at least 1 hour for the flavors to blend. (The mayonnaise can be prepared up to 3 days ahead of serving, covered and refrigerated. Serve at room temperature.) Makes about 1 cup.

2. Melt enough vegetable shortening in a metal fondue pot to come halfway up the sides. Heat on the kitchen stove over high heat until a deep-frying thermometer reads 375°F. Transfer the pot to a fondue burner with a high flame.

3. Allow guests to cook their swordfish just until browned around the edges—do not overcook. Serve with the tapenade mayonnaise, along with any additional sauces.

Shellfish Fondue with Tartar Sauce

makes 4 to 6 servings

IT'S SO HARD to decide what single shellfish to "fondue" that I normally offer an assortment. Shrimp, squid, scallops, and clams are my favorites.

Tartar Sauce

1 cup Homemade Mayonnaise
    (page 82), or store-bought

2 scallions, white and green
    parts, finely chopped

2 tablespoons finely chopped
    cornichons (tiny French pickles) or dill pickles

2 tablespoons finely chopped, rinsed bottled capers
    (if nonpareil, leave whole)

2 tablespoons finely chopped fresh parsley

Vegetable shortening, for deep-frying

1 pound large shrimp, peeled, deveined, and butterflied
    (see page 99)

8 ounces sea scallops (if large, cut into ¾-inch cubes)

6 ounces squid, cleaned, bodies cut into ¼-inch-wide
    rings, tentacles coarsely chopped

12 cherrystone clams, shucked

Other Sauces

Aioli (page 83) • Homemade Cocktail Sauce (page 85) • Remoulade Sauce (page 83) • Soy-Chile Dipping Sauce (page 91) • Sweet and Tangy Dipping Sauce (page 91)

1. To make the tartar sauce, mix the mayonnaise, scallions, cornichons, capers, and parsley. Cover and let stand at room temperature for 1 hour. (The sauce can be prepared up to 2

days ahead, covered and refrigerated. Serve at room temperature.) Makes about 1 cup.

2. Melt enough vegetable shortening in a metal fondue pot to come halfway up the sides. Heat on the kitchen stove over high heat until a deep-frying thermometer reads 375°F. Transfer the pot to a fondue burner with a high flame.

3. Allow guests to cook their shellfish just until cooked through. Take special care not to overcook the squid, or it will become tough. Serve with the tartar sauce, along with any additional sauces.

Rosemary Bagna Cauda
with Vegetables

B*AGNA CAUDA* ("hot bath") is one of the most popular northern Italian dishes, especially in the autumn
when vegetables are still abundant, but there is a nip in the air.
The original recipe is only oil, garlic, and anchovies, but I find
rosemary and peppers round out the flavor. It is a great light
meal to share with friends who prefer vegetables over meat,
but there are some details. First, if your friends are totally
vegetarian, note that *bagna cauda* includes anchovies
(although it is feasible to leave them out). Second, have the
vegetables thoroughly chilled, as they will help cool off the
hot oil and help keep your guests from accidentally burning
their mouths, And finally, whoever
those friends are, they had better all
love garlic!

2 cups extra-virgin olive oil

6 anchovy fillets in oil, drained
and finely chopped

4 garlic cloves, finely chopped

4 (3-inch) sprigs of fresh
rosemary

2 whole dried hot red chiles or
½ teaspoon crushed hot red
pepper flakes

What to Dip

Crusty Italian bread, sliced
(not cut into cubes) or
breadsticks • Focaccia,
cut into 2-inch squares •
Raw carrot sticks • Raw
celery sticks • Cherry
tomatoes • Raw zucchini
sticks • Raw small mush-
room caps • Raw red bell
pepper strips • Broccoli
or cauliflower florets,
prepared for dipping
(see page 14)

1. In a metal fondue pot, heat 2 tablespoons of the oil over medium-low heat. Add the anchovies and garlic and cook, stirring constantly, until the garlic softens and the anchovies dissolve into a paste, about 2 minutes. Add the remaining oil, rosemary, and chiles. Cook slowly just until the oil is warm, about 5 minutes. Remove from the heat and let the bagna cauda stand for 30 minutes.

2. When ready to serve, reheat the *bagna cauda* over low heat until just warm. Transfer to a metal fondue pot and keep warm over a low flame. Serve with the dipping ingredients of your choice.

Homemade Mayonnaise

MAYONNAISE IS THE portal to many a fine fondue sauce. Sure, you could use store-bought mayonnaise, but the homemade version is so easy to whip up in a
blender (plus it tastes so much better). Here are a few tips for
foolproof mayonnaise:

- If you are concerned about using raw eggs, substitute
  ½ cup liquid egg substitute (it's pasteurized and
  salmonella-free), at room temperature, for the eggs.

- The eggs must be at room temperature to emulsify
  properly with the oil. The best, quickest, and safest
  method is to place the chilled, unshelled eggs in a bowl,
  cover with hot tap water, and let stand for 5 minutes.

- The oil should be added to the blender in a slow stream
  —it should take about 1 minute from start to finish.

- Mayonnaise can also be prepared in a food processor
  fitted with the metal blade. Because a food processor
  has twice the RPMs of a blender, it makes a better
  emulsion and the mayonnaise needs an additional
  ¼ cup of vegetable oil to reach the proper thickness.

- Don't think that more olive oil will make better mayonnaise. In fact, it will make the mayonnaise taste heavy
  and cause curdling.

2 large eggs, at room temperature

1 tablespoon fresh lemon juice

2 teaspoons Dijon mustard

½ teaspoon salt

⅛ teaspoon freshly ground pepper

1 cup vegetable oil

½ cup extra-virgin olive oil

1. Place the eggs, lemon juice, mustard, salt, and pepper in the blender. In a glass measuring cup, combine the vegetable and olive oils.

2. With the machine running, slowly add the oils through the opening in the blender lid, and process until the mayonnaise is thick. (The mayonnaise, and all of the following sauces, can be prepared up to 2 days ahead, covered and refrigerated.)

Aioli: For all fondues. Mix 1 cup Homemade Mayonnaise with 1 garlic clove, crushed through a press. Makes about 1 cup.

Aioli with Anchovy and Rosemary: For lamb, swordfish, and shellfish. Mix 1 cup Aioli with 6 anchovy fillets, mashed to a paste, and 1 tablespoon chopped fresh rosemary (or 1½ teaspoons crumbled dried rosemary). Makes a generous 1 cup.

Remoulade Sauce: For shellfish. Mix ½ cup Homemade Mayonnaise, ⅓ cup finely chopped celery with leaves, 1½ tablespoons prepared horseradish, 1 tablespoon minced shallot, 1 tablespoon Creole or spicy brown mustard, 1 tablespoon catsup, and 1 small garlic clove, crushed through a press. Makes about 1¼ cups.

continued

Guacamole Mayonnaise: For chicken, shellfish, and pork. Mix 1 ripe pitted, peeled, and mashed avocado, ½ cup Homemade Mayonnaise, ½ cup sour cream, 1 minced scallion (green and white parts), 1 ripe seeded and minced plum tomato, 1 tablespoon minced fresh cilantro, 1 teaspoon seeded and minced jalapeño, 1 garlic clove, crushed through a press, and ½ teaspoon salt. Makes about 1¾ cups.

Roquefort Mayonnaise: For beef and lamb. Mix ½ cup Homemade Mayonnaise, ½ cup sour cream, 3 ounces crumbled Roquefort or other blue cheese, and ¼ teaspoon freshly ground pepper. Makes about 1⅓ cups.

Pesto Mayonnaise: For beef, chicken, lamb, shellfish, and swordfish. Mix 1 cup Homemade Mayonnaise, ¼ cup minced fresh basil, 2 tablespoons freshly grated Parmigiano-Reggiano cheese, 1 teaspoon fresh lemon juice, 1 garlic clove, crushed through a press, ⅛ teaspoon salt, and ⅛ teaspoon freshly ground pepper. Makes about 1⅓ cups.

Homemade Cocktail Sauce

makes about 1¼ cups

IRRESISTIBLE WITH SHRIMP fondue.

- **1 cup prepared American-style chili sauce**
- **1 small celery rib with leaves, minced**
- **1 tablespoon prepared horseradish**
- **1 tablespoon fresh lemon juice**
- **1 tablespoon finely chopped fresh parsley**
- **1 tablespoon vodka or gin (optional)**

1. In a small bowl, combine the chili sauce, celery, horseradish, lemon juice, parsley, and optional vodka.

2. Cover and let stand for 1 hour for the flavors to blend. (The sauce can be prepared up to 3 days ahead, covered and refrigerated. Serve at room temperature.)

Ginger Dipping Sauce

makes about 1 cup

WITH TERIYAKI-LIKE OVERTONES, this thin dipping sauce is an easy way to bring Asian flavors to just about any fondue—it seems to go with everything, from beef to shellfish. Serve it in individual ramekins.

> ¼ cup shredded fresh ginger (use the large holes of a
>   cheese grater)
> ¼ cup soy sauce, preferably Japanese
> ¼ cup sweet sherry, such as oloroso
> ¼ cup rice vinegar
> 1 tablespoon light brown sugar

1. In a small bowl, combine the ginger, soy sauce, sherry, rice vinegar, and brown sugar, stirring to dissolve the sugar.

2. Cover and let stand at room temperature for 1 hour for the flavors to blend. (The sauce can be prepared up to 1 day ahead, stored at room temperature.)

Easy Peanut Sauce

makes about ¾ cup

JUST A FEW years ago, this Southeast Asian sauce was considered quite unusual, but now is enjoyed all over the states.

⅓ cup chicken broth, preferably homemade, or use low-sodium canned broth

¼ cup unsalted peanut butter, preferably chunky

¼ cup hoisin sauce

1 tablespoon Asian fish sauce (see Note)

½ teaspoon Chinese chili paste with garlic

1. In a small bowl, mix the broth, peanut butter, hoisin sauce, fish sauce, and chili paste until combined.

2. Cover and let stand at room temperature for 30 minutes for the flavors to blend. (The sauce can be prepared up to 1 day ahead, covered and refrigerated. Thin to desired consistency with additional broth or water. Serve at room temperature.)

Note: Fish sauce, also known as *nam pla* or *nuoc mam*, is a quintessential Southeast Asian seasoning. It is available at Asian grocers and many supermarkets. If necessary, substitute equal parts (1 teaspoon each) Worcestershire sauce, soy sauce, and water.

Greek Yogurt and Cucumber Sauce

makes about 1 ¼ cups

YOGURT AND CUCUMBERS both have excess liquid that must be drained so the sauce can stay thick without "weeping." Try this sauce with lamb, chicken, or swordfish.

2 cups plain low-fat yogurt

1 medium cucumber

½ plus ⅛ teaspoon salt

1 scallion, white and green parts, finely chopped

1 tablespoon finely chopped fresh dill

1 garlic clove, crushed through a press

¼ teaspoon ground cumin

Pinch of cayenne pepper

1. Place the yogurt in a paper towel–lined sieve set over a large bowl—the bottom of the bowl should clear the bottom of the sieve by at least 2 inches. Place a saucer on top of the yogurt to weigh it down slightly. Let stand at room temperature for 1 hour. About 1 cup of the whey should drain off. Discard the whey. Place the drained yogurt in a medium bowl.

2. Meanwhile, peel the cucumber, split it lengthwise, and scoop out the seeds. Coarsely chop the cucumber. In a food processor fitted with the metal chopping blade, pulse the cucumber 8 to 10 times, until finely chopped but not puréed. Transfer to a medium bowl and toss with ½ teaspoon salt. Let stand for 1 hour. Drain into a wire sieve and rinse well under

cold running water to remove the salt. Drain well. A handful at a time, squeeze the cucumber well to remove excess liquid, then stir the cucumber into the yogurt.

3. Stir in the scallion, dill, garlic, cumin, remaining ⅛ teaspoon salt, and cayenne. Cover and refrigerate for 1 hour for the flavors to blend. Serve slightly chilled.

Hot and Sweet Mustard

makes a generous ½ cup

THERE ARE SOME recipes that my friends always ask for, but they're so easy, I'm almost embarrassed to give them out. This is one (and the Apple Butter Mustard on page 68 is another). In the fondue world, it is great with sausage and pork.

⅓ cup prepared Chinese mustard
⅓ cup honey

1. In a small bowl, mix the mustard and honey until smooth.

2. Cover and let stand at room temperature for 1 hour for the flavors to blend. (The sauce can be prepared up to 3 days ahead, covered and refrigerated. Serve at room temperature.)

Roasted Red Pepper and Almond Sauce

makes about ¾ cup

WITH MORE THAN a passing resemblance to the Spanish red pepper sauce, *romesco*, this sauce is a zesty accompaniment to lamb, pork, swordfish, or shellfish.

1 large red bell pepper

⅓ cup sliced almonds

1 teaspoon fresh lemon juice

1 garlic clove, crushed through a press

½ cup Homemade Mayonnaise (page 82)

½ teaspoon sweet paprika

¼ teaspoon ground cumin

¼ teaspoon salt

Hot red pepper sauce, to taste

1. Roast the pepper, turning often, sitting directly over a gas flame or under a broiler, until the skin is completely charred. Place in a bowl and cover tightly with plastic wrap. Let steam for 15 minutes. Remove the charred skin, stem, ribs, and seeds. Only if necessary to help clean it, quickly rinse the pepper under cold running water.

2. Heat a medium skillet over medium heat. Add the almonds and cook, stirring occasionally, until toasted, about 3 minutes. Transfer to a plate to cool completely.

3. In a food processor fitted with the metal blade, or a blender, process the roasted pepper, almonds, lemon juice, and garlic until very finely chopped. Transfer to a small bowl.

Stir in the mayonnaise, paprika, cumin, and salt. Season with the hot pepper sauce. Cover and let stand at room temperature for 1 hour to blend the flavors. (The sauce can be prepared up to 3 days ahead, covered and refrigerated. Serve at room temperature.)

Sweet and Tangy Dipping Sauce

makes about ⅔ cup

DELICIOUS WITH SHELLFISH fondue, especially squid. The Soy-Chile Dipping Sauce variation is similar, but a bit milder, lacking garlic. Both sauces should be served in ramekins or custard cups.

¼ cup Asian fish sauce (see Note, page 87)
¼ cup fresh lime juice
1 tablespoon light brown sugar
2 garlic cloves, minced
1 teaspoon crushed hot red pepper flakes

1. In a small bowl, mix the fish sauce, lime juice, brown sugar, garlic, and red pepper flakes, stirring to dissolve the sugar.

2. Cover and let stand at room temperature for 1 hour to blend the flavors. (The sauce can be prepared up to 2 days ahead, covered and refrigerated. Serve at room temperature.)

Soy-Chile Dipping Sauce: Mix ½ cup Japanese soy sauce, ¼ cup rice vinegar, and 2 teaspoons hot chile oil. Makes about ¾ cup.

Quick BBQ Sauce

makes about 1 cup

EVERYONE LOVES BBQ. This sauce is great with anything that can be barbecued, which doesn't leave much out.

> 1 tablespoon unsalted butter
>
> ⅓ cup finely chopped onion
>
> 1 garlic clove, crushed through a press
>
> 1 cup American-style chili sauce
>
> 2 tablespoons fresh lemon juice
>
> 2 tablespoons Worcestershire sauce
>
> 2 tablespoons light brown sugar
>
> Grated zest of 1 lemon
>
> Hot red pepper sauce, to taste

1. In a small saucepan, melt the butter over medium-low heat. Add the onion and cook, stirring often, until golden, about 6 minutes. Stir in the garlic and cook until fragrant, about 1 minute.

2. Stir in the chili sauce, lemon juice, Worcestershire sauce, sugar, and zest. Reduce the heat to very low and simmer, stirring often to avoid scorching, until the sauce is thickened, about 15 minutes. Season with the hot sauce. Cool to room temperature. (The sauce can be prepared, cooled, covered, and refrigerated, up to 3 days ahead. Serve at room temperature.)

The Asian
Hot Pot Family

THE tradition of communal meals served from a simmering pot runs through Asian cuisine. The Chinese call their version hot pot or fire pot. Japanese cooks call all one-pot simmered dishes *nabemono*. Vietnamese beef "fondue" in rice vinegar broth (*bo nung dam*) is considered an extra-special dish, reserved for birthdays and holidays. Even though I don't provide a recipe for it (being somewhat time-consuming in its preparation of tiny meatballs and egg omelets), Koreans love their hot pot, *sin-seon-lo*. Many cooks call these dishes "Asian fondue," or "fondue Chinoise." I am hardly an etymologist, but I prefer to call them Asian hot pots. Fondue is a Western dish with its own customs, and the venerable Eastern hot pot deserves its own separate class.

Throughout this chapter, I refer to "Asian housewares stores" and "Asian grocers." Just a few years ago, if I wanted to buy a hot pot or lemongrass, it meant a trip to the Asian section (Chinatown) of a large American city. As I travel all over the country teaching cooking classes, I have been surprised to see how the recent influx of Asians has affected the marketplace. Japanese, Thai, Vietnamese, Korean, and of course Chinese foods and cooking utensils are not the exotica they used to be. I spend much of my time in suburban California, and shopping at my neighborhood Safeway is a multicultural experience. If you don't know exactly where to find these stores in your area, call your local cooking school and ask them—I'll bet they'll know.

Equipment

A Chinese hot pot looks somewhat like a chafing dish with a chimney in the center. The cooking bowl sits on a stand that holds the heating fuel. The cooking bowl can be used on the stove to bring the stock to a simmer (although I usually use a regular saucepan for this step, and transfer it to the hot pot). The hot pot has a lid that holds the heat in while the guests are resting between "dips." Hot pots can be made of bronze, stainless steel, or copper. There are electric hot pots, too, and like electric fondue pots, they will appeal to the most practical cooks. Hot pots can be found at Asian housewares stores and markets. If you don't have a hot pot, simply use a metal fondue pot.

In Asia, hot pots are usually heated by dropping ignited charcoal into the chimney. American cooks will certainly prefer heating their hot pots with a can of heating fuel placed in the stand—the flame will shoot up into the chimney, heating it just as the briquettes would. Not only is the canned heating fuel more efficient and easier to handle, it is dangerous to breathe charcoal fumes in an enclosed, unventilated space. Many Asian kitchens are outdoors, so this isn't such a problem. Also, Asian cooks would use untreated hardwood charcoal, not our charcoal briquettes, which are held together with petroleum gums that give off more air pollutants. No matter how you cut it, unless you are eating outdoors and can handle transferring live coals to the hot pot, use the canned heating fuel and don't try to be a hero.

The recipes in this chapter were devised to be eaten in the Asian manner—that is, with chopsticks, not fondue forks. Chinese diners often use small dipping baskets to hold their food. These baskets are available at the stores that sell the hot pots themselves.

Ingredients

Stock: There are two schools of thought concerning hot pot stock. The first is that the better the stock, the better the hot pot—and the best stock is homemade. The argument for homemade stock becomes stronger considering how little actual hands-on time it takes to make. Most canned broths have carrots, herbs, and other ingredients that are most appropriate for Western recipes. I usually make my own hot pot stock, seasoned with ginger and scallions for Asian flavor. Hot pot stock should be lightly flavored, not the meaty powerhouse that some Western chefs prefer. Asian Chicken Stock (page 105) is the best all-purpose choice, but meat or seafood hot pots will be enhanced if served with an appropriate stock made from the same ingredients. Try to make homemade stocks far enough ahead of serving that the stock can be chilled—any fat will solidify on the surface and can be scraped off. If you're in a hurry, let the hot, strained stock stand for 5 minutes, then skim the clear yellow fat from the surface, and skip the cooling and refrigerating steps.

More practical cooks use a good canned stock, realizing its flavor will be improved as the different vegetables and meats are dipped into it. Reduced-sodium canned broths have the best flavor. While traveling and teaching at cooking schools around the country, I have come across some excellent broths, either canned or frozen (found at fine butchers and gourmet food stores).

In Japan, *nabemono* dishes often use *dashi*, a seaweed-and-dried fish broth that is as important to their cuisine as meat or poultry stock is to ours. Western cooks will find chicken or seafood stocks to be fine substitutes. Asian ingredients are becoming easier to find than before (I can buy dashi seaweed at my health food store, or instant dashi at my corner grocery), and a dashi recipe is included for those who would like to experience a true taste of Japan.

Meats, Poultry, and Fish: Whether you choose to serve meat (beef, pork, or lamb), poultry (chicken, turkey, or duck breast), fish (skinless firm-fleshed fish, such as snapper, bass, cod, grouper, tilefish, or monkfish) or shellfish (peeled and deveined shrimp; shelled oysters, clams, or mussels), the food must be thinly sliced or cut into bite-sized pieces, so it will cook quickly in the simmering broth. Guest shouldn't have to wait forever to cook their portions. Allow 6 to 8 ounces of boneless food per person.

Choose meats that have a single muscle structure with little gristle and fat—this will keep trimming down and give evenly shaped slices. The best choices (all boneless, and in the case of the poultry, skinless, too) are beef tenderloin, lamb loin, center-cut pork loin, chicken breast, and turkey breast. These are pricy cuts, most easily found at the best butchers, but the waste will be minimal.

Meats and poultry should be cut as thin as possible. If you live near an Asian butcher, the freezer department will often have packages of thinly sliced meats for hot pots. Unfortunately, I have found that these packages are often freezer-burned, and it is often better to do the slicing yourself at home. If you want the butcher to slice the meat, give him plenty of notice, as the meat must be partially frozen to facilitate slicing. After the meat, poultry, fish, or shellfish is prepared, it should be tightly covered or wrapped in plastic and refrigerated until serving.

To slice meat for hot pot cooking, use a thin, sharp knife to trim away the fat and gristle, along with any membrane that may be covering the meat. Wrap in plastic wrap and freeze until firm and partially frozen, 1 to 2 hours depending on the thickness of the meat and the freezer's temperature. Unwrap the meat and use a thin, sharp knife to cut across the grain into slices as thin as possible. Wrap the slices tightly in plastic wrap and refrigerate until ready to serve.

For Mongolian lamb hot pot, it is possible to use leg of

lamb instead of lamb loin, if it is prepared carefully. Most American butchers cut across a piece of meat, through the bone, often giving several different muscles in a single steak. European and Asian butchers have a different technique that follows the animal's natural muscle structure around the bone. With a large leg of lamb that hasn't been cut up, you will have more control over the procedure. Ask the butcher to bone the lamb, but not to butterfly it. When you get the lamb home, use a long, thin, sharp knife to trim away the surface fat covering the outside of the lamb. The lamb is composed of muscle groups that run the length of the leg bone. The idea is to separate these muscles from each other, keeping them as intact as possible. Use the knife to separate the muscle groups from each other, cutting them apart where the seams of gristle occur (professionals call this "seaming" the meat). Trim away any thin gristle covering the pieces of meat, and discard any extraneous fat. If you have an excellent butcher who will seam the meat for you, so much the better.

To slice poultry for hot pot cooking, use skinless, boneless turkey or chicken breast. Wrap and freeze until firm and partially frozen. Hold a thin, sharp knife at a 45° angle, and slice the meat across the grain into thin, wide slices. (Holding the knife at an angle makes slices wider than cutting straight down.)

To prepare fish for hot pot cooking, simply cut the fish fillets into bite-sized pieces. Avoid salmon, bluefish, mackerel, and other strong-flavored, oily fishes, as they will make the stock too strong.

To prepare oysters and clams, shuck the shellfish, reserving any juices (or have the fish store do this). Place the shucked shellfish in individual bowls with their juices to help keep them moist before serving. Large sea scallops should be cut into bite-sized pieces. The smaller bay scallops are often too small to bother with.

To prepare shrimp, peel and devein the shrimp. The shrimp should be butterflied for quicker cooking. Following the vein incision, cut almost through to the other side, and spread the two flaps open.

Vegetables and Noodles: Each particular recipe gives ingredients used in the dish's traditional version, but let your personal imagination and color sense contribute to the platter scheme. In China, the platter is usually garnished with chrysanthemum blossoms and leaves. If you have any unsprayed flowers in your garden that will be attractive, use them as a garnish—they are not meant to be eaten.

Bamboo Shoots: Use canned, thinly sliced bamboo shoots, rinsed and drained.

Bean Sprouts: Rinse well and pluck off the darkened "heads."

Bean Threads: These very thin, white noodles are also called cellophane noodles, *sai fun*, and bean vermicelli. They come bundled into 1- to 2-ounce skeins. It is best to prepare them just before serving. Place the bean threads in a large bowl and cover with hot tap water. Let stand until softened, about 10 minutes. Drain well. Snip through the cooked noodles a few times with kitchen scissors, as they are usually too long to manage easily. Bean threads can either be cooked along with the meat and vegetables, or stirred into the broth at the end of the meal to serve as a soup course.

Cabbage and Spinach Rolls: These elegant rolls are really very easy to make—the procedure only seems long because it is unfamiliar to Western cooks and necessarily detailed.

Bring a large pot of lightly salted water to a boil over high heat. Add 6 large, outer leaves of napa cabbage and cook just until wilted, about 1 minute. Using a large skimmer or slotted spoon, transfer to a colander, rinse under cold water until cool, then drain well. Place 2 cabbage leaves on top of each other, with the thick stem of each leaf going in a different direction than the other. Starting at a long end, roll up the leaves together and squeeze firmly to remove excess water. Set aside. Repeat with the other leaves to make 3 portions.

Return the water to a full boil. Add 8 ounces of trimmed, rinsed spinach leaves, and cook just until wilted, about 1 minute. Using the skimmer, transfer to a colander and rinse under cold running water until cool. Drain well. A handful at a time, squeeze out the excess water from the spinach and place in a bowl.

Unroll 1 cabbage roll with the long side facing you, and place on a bamboo sushi mat or a clean kitchen towel. Arrange one-third of the spinach on the cabbage, leaving a ½-inch border at the top and bottom. Fold in the cabbage about ½ inch at each side. Starting at the long side facing you, and using the mat or the towel as an aid, roll up the cabbage to enclose the spinach and make a tight cylinder. Squeeze the mat or towel to remove any remaining moisture. Wrap the cabbage roll in plastic wrap. Repeat with the remaining ingredients. Refrigerate for at least 1 hour or up to 1 day. Unwrap and cut crosswise into ½-to ¾-inch-thick rounds.

Carrots: Peel the carrots. Using a sharp knife, diagonally cut into very thin slices. Bring a large pot of lightly salted water to a boil. Add the carrot slices and cook just until the color is set, about 1 minute. Drain and rinse under cold running water.

Cucumbers: If possible, use Kirby or pickling cucumbers

that have not been waxed. These need only to be scrubbed and are unnecessary to peel. Otherwise, peel regular cucumbers. Cut the cucumber in half lengthwise. Using the tip of a dessert spoon, scoop out the seeds. Cut each cucumber into ⅛-inch-thick half-moons.

Daikon: Also called white radish. Peel the daikon, and using a mandoline or a sharp knife, cut into very thin rounds.

Egg Noodles, Chinese: Available fresh or dried at Asian grocers. To prepare, bring a large pot of lightly salted water to a boil over high heat. Add the noodles and cook until tender, about 3 minutes for fresh noodles or 9 minutes for dried. Drain and rinse under cold running water. If not serving immediately, toss with 1 teaspoon dark Asian sesame oil to discourage sticking. If necessary, substitute fresh or dried linguine.

Enoki Mushrooms: These thin, long-stemmed white mushrooms can be found in Asian groceries and many supermarkets. They have a delicate flavor. Trim off the cluster at the end of the bunch. Rinse the bunch quickly under cold running water to remove any grit.

Napa Cabbage: Also called Chinese cabbage. Use the large outer leaves, and cut into large pieces, about 2 inches square.

Onions, Browned: Browned onions are served as part of the Sukiyaki Hot Pot (page 116) platter. Slice a large onion in half, then cut into thin half-moons. In a large skillet, heat 1 tablespoon of vegetable oil. Add the onion and cook, stirring often, until golden brown, about 7 minutes. The onion can be served at chilled or at room temperature, as it will be reheated in the simmering broth.

Rice Vermicelli: Also called *bahn pho* or "rice sticks." These come in various widths, but for Vietnamese Beef

"Fondue" (page 117), the thinnest width (about ¹⁄₁₆ inch) is preferred. Place the noodles in a large bowl, and add enough cold water to cover. Let stand until softened, about 10 minutes. Drain well. Using kitchen shears, snip through the rice noodles to coarsely chop. Rice vermicelli is best prepared just before serving.

Scallions: Trim the ends and cut into 1½-inch lengths.

Shiitake Mushrooms: Very quickly rinse the mushrooms under cold running water to remove any grit and drain well. Pat the mushrooms dry with paper towels. Cut off and discard the stems, which are tough and inedible. Cut the mushroom caps into ½-inch-wide strips.

Spinach: Use young, tender spinach with smooth leaves, not crinkled, cellophane-wrapped spinach. Trim off the stems and discard. Fill a sink or a large bowl with cold water. Place the spinach in the water and agitate well to remove grit. Lift out the spinach and transfer to a large colander, leaving the grit behind to sink to the bottom of the water. Taste a piece of spinach, and if it is still gritty, repeat the rinsing procedure.

Tofu: Use firm tofu. Cut the drained tofu into bite-sized cubes, about ¾-inch square.

Udon: Thick Japanese wheat noodles, made without eggs. They are available at Asian grocers and many supermarkets, either fresh or dried. To prepare, bring a large pot of lightly salted water to a boil over high heat. Add the udon and cook until tender, about 3 minutes for fresh udon, and 9 minutes for dried. Drain and rinse under cold running water. If not serving immediately, toss with 1 teaspoon dark Asian sesame oil to discourage sticking. If necessary, substitute fresh or dried fettuccine (which is made with eggs, but is a reasonable substitute). Udon are usually stirred into broth after the meat and vegetables have been cooked, and served as a soup course.

Watercress: Rinse well and cut off any tough stems.

Serving Asian Hot Pots

Regardless of country of origin or name, a portable burner with large pot of simmering broth is set in the center of the table, and a platter of artfully arranged raw ingredients placed alongside. Each diner picks up a morsel with his or her chopsticks, submerges it into the hot broth to cook (as the ingredients are thinly sliced, this only takes a few seconds), dips it into a seasoning sauce, and eats it. The broth's flavor is enhanced by the assorted vegetables and meats cooked in it. When all the ingredients have been cooked, this delicious stock is sipped by itself as a soup, or bolstered with the addition of previously cooked noodles.

The hot pot should be placed on a thick trivet to protect the table. Provide each diner with a pair of chopsticks or a small hot pot dipping basket; a dinner plate; an empty bowl for serving the soup; a soup spoon; a bowl of rice when suggested; and a small bowl of the dipping sauce. The dipping sauce bowl can be a custard cup or a ramekin, but authentic Asian dipping bowls are very inexpensive and can be found at any Asian housewares store and many Asian grocers.

Variety is the key to a successful hot pot dinner. The ingredients are chosen not only for taste but also for contrast in color and texture. Whenever I bring out a platter (or two) of food, ready for simmering, my guests always gasp in admiration. Imagine an arrangement of jade green spinach rolled inside of pale napa cabbage leaves, ivory enoki mushrooms, vibrant orange carrots, tangles of bean thread noodles, a mound of thinly sliced raw beef, shrimp, or chicken, and a bunch of watercress. Even though the entire affair took hardly any time to prepare, it translates into a sense of abundance and well-being. And speaking of well-being, Asian hot pots are excellent meals to serve to guests who are trimming fat out of their diet.

While each hot pot has its classic ingredients, the traditional recipes should be considered a point of departure, rather than an edict. Mix and match according to taste and availability. On the other hand, these recipes are best when served with the suggested dipping sauce. (Hot oil fondues are served with a selection of sauces, but not hot pots.)

One last serving suggestion. Six or eight large leaves of napa cabbage make a sufficient amount for a platter. I usually turn the leftover cabbage into an Asian slaw (page 111) to round out the meal, serving it at the same time as the hot pot.

Fondue Great Food to Dip, Dunk, Savor, and Swirl

Asian Chicken Stock

H ERE'S A BASIC stock that can be used for any of the recipes in this chapter. Inexpensive chicken backs can be used instead of, or in addition to, the wings, but be sure to chop them into three or four pieces so they can release their flavor more efficiently.

2 pounds chicken wings

2 scallions, white and green parts, coarsely chopped

2 ⅛-inch-thick slices of fresh ginger, crushed under a knife

2 garlic cloves, crushed under a knife

6 whole peppercorns

½ teaspoon salt

1. Using a cleaver or a heavy knife, chop the chicken wings at the joints. (Or ask the butcher to chop them for you.)

2. Place the wings in a large saucepan and add 2 quarts of water. Bring to a boil over high heat, skimming off any foam that rises to the surface. Add the scallions, ginger, garlic, and peppercorns. Reduce the heat to very low and simmer until full-flavored, 2 to 3 hours, the longer the better. Season with the salt.

3. Strain into a large bowl and let cool to room temperature. Refrigerate until chilled, at least 3 hours. Using a large spoon, scrape off the fat that rises to the surface. (The stock can be prepared, covered and refrigerated, for 2 days before serving.)

continued

Quick Asian Chicken Stock: In a large saucepan, bring 6 cups canned reduced-sodium chicken broth, 2 chopped scallions, 1 tablespoon shredded fresh ginger, 2 minced garlic cloves, and 6 peppercorns to a simmer over medium heat. Remove from the heat and let stand for 30 minutes. Strain.

Asian Beef Stock

makes about 1½ quarts

BEEF-BASED HOT POTS, like *shabu-shabu*, get a boost of flavor when prepared with this stock. Soy sauce not only seasons the stock but also deepens the color. It is important to use a Japanese soy sauce, as the saltiness of other varieties is inconsistent.

> 2½ pounds beef bones, sawed into pieces
>
> 2 scallions, white and green parts, coarsely chopped
>
> 2⅛-inch-thick slices of fresh ginger, crushed under a knife
>
> 2 garlic cloves, crushed under a knife
>
> 6 whole peppercorns
>
> 1 tablespoon Japanese soy sauce
>
> ¼ teaspoon salt

1. Position a broiler rack about 6 inches from the source of heat and preheat the broiler. Broil the bones, turning occasionally, until browned on all sides, 10 to 15 minutes.

 Fondue **Great Food to Dip, Dunk, Savor, and Swirl**

2. Place the browned bones in a large saucepan, and add 2 quarts of water. Bring to a boil over high heat, skimming off any foam that rises to the surface. Add the scallions, ginger, garlic, and peppercorns. Reduce the heat to very low and simmer until full-flavored, 3 to 4 hours, the longer the better. Season with the soy sauce and salt.

3. Strain into a large bowl and let cool to room temperature. Refrigerate until chilled, at least 3 hours. Using a large spoon, scrape off the fat that rises to the surface. (The stock can be prepared, covered and refrigerated, for 2 days before serving.)

Quick Asian Beef Stock: In a large saucepan, bring 6 cups canned reduced-sodium beef broth, 2 chopped scallions, 1 tablespoon shredded fresh ginger, 2 minced garlic cloves, 1 tablespoon soy sauce, 1/4 teaspoon salt, and 6 peppercorns to a simmer over medium heat. Remove from the heat and let stand for 30 minutes. Strain.

Asian Lamb Stock: Substitute 2½ pounds lamb bones (lamb neck, or the bones from a boned leg of lamb, sawed by the butcher into pieces) for the beef bones.

Asian Fish Stock

makes about 1½ quarts

ASK YOUR FISHMONGER for head, bones, and trimmings from nonoily, white-fleshed fish—salmon, bluefish, and mackerel bones are too strong to make a good-tasting stock. Unfortunately, supermarkets are not in the habit of stocking fish bones and trimmings, so many cooks may have to settle for the Quick Asian Fish Stock. Fish bones are delicate, and need only 30 minutes to give off their flavor into a stock.

1½ pounds heads, bones, and trimmings (no gills) from white-fleshed fish such as snapper, bass, or cod

½ cup sake or dry sherry

2 scallions, white and green parts, coarsely chopped

2 ⅛-inch-thick slices of fresh ginger, crushed under a knife

8 whole peppercorns

¼ teaspoon salt

1. Place the fish bones in a large bowl and add enough cold water to cover. Let stand for 30 minutes. (This refreshes the bones and makes a clearer stock.) Drain.

2. Transfer the drained bones to a large saucepan and add 2 quarts fresh water and the sake. Bring to a boil over high heat, skimming off any foam that rises to the surface. Add the scallions, ginger, and peppercorns. Reduce the heat to very low and simmer until full-flavored, about 30 minutes. Season with the salt.

3. Strain into a large bowl and let cool to room temperature. (The stock can be prepared, covered and refrigerated, for 1 day before serving.)

Quick Asian Fish Stock: In a large saucepan, bring 3 cups bottled clam juice, 3 cups water, ¼ cup sake or dry sherry, 2 chopped scallions, 1 tablespoon shredded fresh ginger, 1 minced garlic clove, ¼ teaspoon salt, and 6 peppercorns to a simmer over high heat. Remove from the heat and let stand for 30 minutes. Strain.

Japanese Sea Stock (Dashi)

makes about 1 ½ quarts

DASHI, PREPARED FROM flaked, dried bonito (related to tuna) and *kombu* (a variety of kelp), has a unique smoky flavor that is also as fresh as an ocean breeze. For many cooks, finding dashi's two essential ingredients may mean a trip to an Asian grocer—for others, especially Californians, it means a trip to the local supermarket or neighborhood natural foods store. Bonito flakes and *kombu* will keep almost indefinitely in a cool, dark cupboard, and with them on hand, you may find yourself cooking other Japanese recipes. There is also instant dashi, which has a better reputation among Japanese cooks than bouillon cubes do in American kitchens, so you may want to try it, following the proportions on the package to make 6 cups.

1 (4-inch) square piece of *kombu* (see Note)

½ cup dried bonito flakes

continued

1. Rinse the *kombu* under cold running water (the white film on the kelp is harmless). Place in a large saucepan and add 6½ cups cold water. Bring to a boil over high heat. As soon as the water comes to a boil, use tongs to remove the *kombu*, which will make the dashi unpleasantly strong if allowed to boil.

2. Stir the bonito flakes into the boiling water and remove from the heat. Let stand for 2 minutes.

3. Strain the dashi through a wire sieve lined with cheesecloth or paper towels. (The dashi can be prepared up to 2 days ahead, cooled, covered, and refrigerated.)

Note: *Kombu* is usually packaged in portions that have been pleated to fit into the bag. When rinsed, these pleated portions will be about 4 inches square, the right amount for 5 to 6 cups of water. If the *kombu* has been packaged flat and unfolded, use scissors to cut it into a 4-inch square.

Fondue **Great Food to Dip, Dunk, Savor, and Swirl**

Asian Cabbage Slaw

makes 6 servings

ONCE THE LARGE outer leaves of a head of napa cabbage are prepared for the hot pot platter, make this delicious slaw from the leftover cabbage.

¼ **cup rice vinegar**

1 **tablespoon dark Asian sesame oil**

1 **teaspoon sugar**

1 **garlic clove, crushed through a press**

½ **teaspoon salt**

¼ **teaspoon freshly ground pepper**

⅔ **cup vegetable oil**

6 **cups thinly shredded napa cabbage**

3 **medium carrots, shredded**

2 **scallions, white and green parts, finely chopped**

2 **tablespoons chopped fresh cilantro (optional)**

¼ **cup chopped unsalted peanuts**

1. In a large bowl, whisk the vinegar, sesame oil, sugar, garlic, salt, and pepper. Gradually whisk in the vegetable oil until combined.

2. Add the cabbage, carrots, scallions, and optional cilantro and toss well. Cover and refrigerate until chilled, at least 1 and up to 6 hours (the slaw will wilt if made more than 6 hours ahead). Just before serving, sprinkle with the peanuts.

Classic Chinese
Chrysanthemum Hot Pot

makes 4 to 6 servings

COOKED CHRYSANTHEMUM BLOSSOMS are not a part of this famous dish. The Chinese consider autumn to be the best time to enjoy this hot pot, and as fall is mum season, too, the flowers are used as a garnish. Whereas other hot pots feature just one kind of meat, a chrysanthemum hot pot should have as many selections as possible. The procedure here is to enjoy the meat, poultry, and seafood selections first, then add the vegetables and noodles to the stock as a soup.

Dipping Sauce

½ cup soy sauce

¼ cup Chinese rice wine or dry sherry

¼ cup dark Asian sesame oil

4 cups Asian Chicken Stock (page 105)

The Meat Platter (prepared according to the instructions on pages 96–98)

½ pound boneless, skinless chicken breast, thinly sliced

½ pound beef tenderloin, thinly sliced

½ pound center-cut pork loin, thinly sliced

½ pound firm, white-fleshed fish filets, cut into bite-sized cubes

½ pound medium shrimp, peeled, deveined, and butterflied

1 dozen shucked cherrystone clams

6 to 8 shucked oysters

Chrysanthemum blossoms and leaves, for garnish

Fondue Great Food to Dip, Dunk, Savor, and Swirl

8 large, outer leaves napa cabbage, cut into 2-inch
   squares

1 (6-ounce) bunch watercress, tough stems removed

4 ounces firm tofu, cut into ¾-inch cubes

2 skeins bean threads, softened, and coarsely chopped

1. To make the dipping sauce, whisk the soy sauce and sherry in a small bowl. Gradually whisk in the sesame oil. Cover and set aside. When ready to serve, transfer the sauce to individual small bowls for dipping.

2. In a large saucepan, bring the stock to a boil over high heat. Transfer to a hot pot or a metal fondue pot and keep at a simmer over a flame.

3. Present the meat platter. Using chopsticks or small hot pot baskets, allow guests to cook their selections in the simmering broth, and dip into their own bowl of dipping sauce.

4. When all of the meat, poultry, and fish have been cooked, add the vegetable and noodle platter. Add the cabbage, spinach, tofu, and bean threads to the stock and cook until heated through, about 1 minute. Ladle the soup into individual bowls and serve, allowing the guests to season the soup with the dipping sauce.

Shabu-Shabu with Sesame Dipping Sauce

THIS JAPANESE hot pot gets its name from the sound the beef makes when swished through the cooking stock. Its dipping sauce is based on toasted, ground sesame seeds. Sesame seeds are very cheap at Asian grocers and natural food stores, but prohibitively expensive when purchased in those little jars at the supermarket.

Sesame Sauce

⅔ cup (about 3 ounces) sesame seeds

¼ cup mirin (see Note) or sweet sherry, such as oloroso

¼ cup Japanese soy sauce

2 tablespoons fresh lime juice

2 tablespoons water

2 teaspoons sugar

4 cups Asian Beef Stock (page 106)

The Platter (prepared according to the instructions on pages 96–103)

2 pounds beef tenderloin, thinly sliced

3 cabbage and spinach rolls, cut into rounds, or

8 large outer leaves napa cabbage, cut into 2-inch squares

12 ounces young, tender leaf spinach, tough stems removed

4 ounces canned sliced bamboo shoots, rinsed and drained

4 ounces thinly sliced daikon

8 fresh shiitake mushrooms, stems removed, caps cut into ½-inch-wide strips

6 scallions, cut into 1½-inch lengths

2 medium carrots, cut on the bias into thin slices, blanched (see page 14)

2 skeins bean threads, softened, and drained

8 ounces firm tofu, cut into bite-sized cubes

Hot cooked rice, for serving

1. To make the sauce, heat an empty skillet over medium heat. Add the sesame seeds and cook, stirring often, until toasted. Immediately transfer to a blender. Add the mirin, soy sauce, lime juice, water, and sugar. Blend until smooth, stopping to stir down the sauce from the sides of the blender container as necessary. Cover and set aside. When ready to serve, transfer the sauce to individual small bowls for dipping.

2. In a large saucepan, bring the stock to a boil over high heat. Transfer to a hot pot or a metal fondue pot and keep at a simmer over a flame.

3. Present the platter. Using chopsticks or small hot pot baskets, allow guests to cook their selections in the simmering broth, and dip into their own bowl of sauce. Serve with bowls of hot cooked rice.

Note: Mirin, available at Asian and Japanese grocers, is a sweetened rice wine used for cooking. Sweet sherry, such as oloroso, is a good substitute.

Sukiyaki Hot Pot

makes 4 to 6 servings

IN JAPANESE HOMES, sukiyaki is often cooked in an electric skillet at the table. I've taken some liberties, keeping the richly seasoned stock and traditional beef and vegetables, but making it more of a hot pot than a skillet dish. Serve the meat and vegetables over hot rice.

Sukiyaki Stock

2 cups Asian Beef Stock (page 106)

⅓ cup Japanese soy sauce

⅓ cup sake or dry sherry

1 tablespoon sugar

The Platter (prepared according to the instructions on pages 96–103)

2 pounds beef tenderloin, thinly sliced

1 large onion, sliced and browned

6 scallions, cut into 1½-inch lengths

8 fresh shiitake mushrooms, stems removed, caps cut into ½-inch-wide strips

2 cups fresh bean sprouts

4 ounces firm tofu, cut into bite-sized cubes

4 ounces canned sliced bamboo shoots, rinsed and drained

1 (6-ounce) bunch watercress, tough stems removed

2 skeins bean threads, softened, and coarsely chopped

Hot cooked rice

1. Prepare the stock in a medium saucepan, bring the beef stock, soy sauce, sake, and sugar to a simmer over medium

 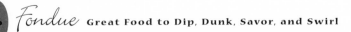

heat. Transfer to a hot pot or metal fondue pot and keep at a simmer over a flame.

2. Present the platter. Using chopsticks or small hot pot baskets, allow guests to cook their selections in the simmering broth. The guests should use the cooked meat and vegetables as a topping for cooked rice, moistening the rice to taste with some of the cooking stock.

Vietnamese Beef "Fondue" with Rice Vinegar Stock and Anchovy-Pineapple Sauce

makes 4 to 6 servings

AS A RULE, fondues are dishes for sharing with friends who like to get into the action, but this Vietnamese specialty calls for more agility than usual from both the host or hostess and guests. The dipped, cooked beef is layered with vegetables and herbs of choice onto rice paper rounds, then rolled up like a burrito. The rice paper rounds must be softened at the table—but it's all part of the fun. A few words of advice: Don't let the amount of vinegar in the stock disconcert you. Rice vinegar is quite mellow and adds a subtle, not strong, sharpness. Also, under all circumstances, leave behind any anti-anchovy feelings and make the dip—it is addictive. Rice paper rounds, rice vermicelli, fish sauce, Thai basil, and Thai peppers can be found at Asian grocers.

continued

Anchovy-Pineapple Sauce

1 (20-ounce) can crushed pineapple in unsweetened juice

¼ cup fresh lime juice

2 tablespoons Asian fish sauce (*nam pla* or *nuoc mam*)

1 tablespoon anchovy paste or minced anchovy fillets

1 tablespoon light brown sugar

2 garlic cloves, minced

1 hot fresh chile, preferably Thai, cut into thin rounds

Rice Vinegar Stock

1 tablespoon vegetable oil

2 tablespoons minced shallots

2 tablespoons minced lemongrass (use the tender bulb
   end only)

1 tablespoon shredded fresh ginger

2 garlic cloves, minced

3 cups Asian Beef Stock (page 106) or Asian Chicken
   Stock (page 105)

½ cup rice vinegar

1 tablespoon light brown sugar

The Platter (prepared according to the instructions on pages 96–103)

1½ pounds beef tenderloin, thinly sliced

1 head Boston lettuce, separated into individual leaves

1 medium cucumber, cut into thin half-moons

1 cup fresh bean sprouts

4 ounces rice vermicelli, softened and coarsely chopped

⅓ cup fresh basil leaves, preferably Thai or holy basil

⅓ cup fresh mint leaves

⅓ cup fresh cilantro leaves

12 to 16 (6½-inch round) rice papers

1. To make the sauce, drain the pineapple well, pressing it gently to extract ½ cup of the juice. Transfer the juice and ¼ cup of the crushed pineapple to a medium bowl. (Save the remaining pineapple for another use.) Stir in the lime juice, fish sauce, anchovy paste, brown sugar, garlic, and chile. Cover and set aside. When ready to serve, transfer the sauce to individual small bowls for dipping.

2. To make the rice vinegar stock, heat the vegetable oil in a medium saucepan over medium heat. Add the shallots, lemongrass, ginger, and garlic and cook, stirring often, until the shallots soften, about 2 minutes. Add the beef stock, rice vinegar, and brown sugar. Bring to a boil over medium heat. Reduce the heat to low and simmer for 10 minutes. Transfer to a hot pot or metal fondue pot and keep at a simmer over a flame.

3. Present the meat and vegetable platter, with the following next to the host's place: a large bowl of warm water, a clean, folded kitchen towel on a plate, and the rice paper rounds.

4. To serve, the host picks up a rice paper round and submerges it in the water. In about 15 seconds, the round will become pliable and transparent. Transfer the round to the kitchen towel and let drain for about 15 seconds. It will soften further. The host passes the softened rice paper round to the first guest. The host repeats the procedure as needed to provide everyone with a rice round. The guests cook their own portions of beef in the simmering stock. To make a roll, place a lettuce leaf on a rice paper round, top with the beef, and small amounts of the other ingredients on the platter. Do not overfill the round or it will crack when rolled (it is just as delicious when eaten with a fork). Fold in the sides of the round, then roll up from the bottom to form a thick cylinder. As the roll is eaten, dip it into the anchovy-pineapple sauce.

Mongolian Lamb Hot Pot with Spicy Dipping Sauce

WHEN I WAS in college in San Francisco, many an evening was spent around a Mongolian hot pot in a Chinese restaurant. In their hot pot, the Mongolians prefer lamb to all other meat, poultry, or fish possibilities. Refer to page 97 for comments on the lamb for this dish—a leg of lamb, if prepared properly, is a good choice, as you will get bones to make a lamb stock. Loin of lamb is less trouble, but lamb bones will have to be purchased for the stock.

Spicy Dipping Sauce

½ cup soy sauce

3 tablespoons rice vinegar

2 tablespoons dark Asian sesame oil

2 tablespoons rice wine or sweet sherry, such as oloroso

1 to 2 teaspoons Chinese chili paste with garlic, to taste

1 teaspoon sugar (optional if using rice wine)

2 tablespoons chopped fresh cilantro, for garnish

Asian Lamb Stock (page 107) or Asian Chicken Stock (page 105)

The Platter (prepared according to the instructions on pages 96–103)

2 pounds boneless lamb, thinly sliced

6 large outer leaves of napa cabbage, cut into 2-inch squares

8 ounces young, tender spinach, tough stems removed, coarsely shredded

8 fresh shiitake mushrooms, stems removed, caps cut
   into ½-inch-thick slices

4 ounces thinly sliced daikon

4 ounces firm tofu, cut into bite-sized cubes

6 scallions, cut into 1½-inch lengths

8 ounces Chinese egg noodles, cooked and drained

1. To make the sauce, in a medium bowl, whisk the soy sauce, vinegar, sesame oil, rice wine, chili paste, and the sugar, if using. Cover and set aside. When ready to serve, transfer the sauce to individual small bowls for dipping, and sprinkle each serving with the cilantro.

2. In a large saucepan, bring the stock to a boil over high heat. Transfer to a hot pot or a metal fondue pot and keep at a simmer over a flame.

3. Present the platter. Using chopsticks or small hot pot baskets, allow guests to cook their selections in the simmering broth, and dip them into their own bowl of sauce.

4. When all of the lamb and vegetables have been cooked, add the egg noodles to the stock and cook until cooked through, about 2 minutes. Ladle the soup into individual bowls and serve, allowing the guests to season the soup with the dipping sauce.

Japanese Chicken and Noodle Hot Pot with Ponzu Dipping Sauce

makes 4 to 6 servings

JAPANESE COOKS KNOW this as *mizutaki*, and it carries the same heartwarming connotations as our chicken noodle soup. It is a good choice for a casual cold-weather supper with friends or family. Ponzu, the tangy soy sauce dip, is available in a bottled version at Japanese grocers, but it is so easy to make, why bother to buy it?

Ponzu Dipping Sauce

½ cup Japanese soy sauce

½ cup fresh lemon juice

2 tablespoons sake or dry sherry

1 teaspoon sugar

4 cups Asian Chicken Stock (page 105)

1 (4-inch square) *kombu* (see page 110), rinsed under cold water (optional)

The Platter (prepared according to the instructions on pages 96–103)

1½ pounds boneless, skinless chicken breasts, thinly sliced

3 cabbage and spinach rolls, cut into rounds, or

8 large outer leaves napa cabbage, cut into 2-inch squares

12 ounces young, tender leaf spinach, tough stems removed

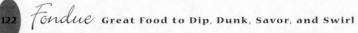

1 (6-ounce) bunch watercress, thick stems removed

4 ounces thinly sliced daikon

8 fresh shiitake mushrooms, stems removed, caps cut
   into ½-inch-wide strips

6 scallions, cut into 1½-inch lengths

2 medium carrots, cut on the bias into thin slices,
   prepared for dipping (see page 14)

8 ounces firm tofu, cut into bite-sized cubes

8 ounces udon, cooked and drained

1. To make the sauce, in a medium bowl, combine the soy sauce, lemon juice, sake, and sugar, stirring to dissolve the sugar. Cover and set aside. When ready to serve, transfer the sauce to individual small bowls for dipping.

2. In a medium saucepan, bring the chicken stock and the optional *kombu* to a boil over high heat. If using the *kombu,* use tongs to remove it as soon as the stock comes to a boil. Transfer the stock to a hot pot or metal fondue pot and keep at a simmer over a flame.

3. Present the platter. Using chopsticks or small hot pot baskets, allow guests to cook their selections in the simmering broth, and dip them into their own bowl of sauce.

4. When all of the chicken and vegetables have been cooked, add the udon to the stock and cook until cooked through, about 2 minutes. Ladle the soup into individual bowls and serve.

Monkfish Hot Pot: When fish is cooked in this manner, it is called *chirinabe.* Substitute Japanese Sea Stock (page 109) or Asian Fish Stock (page 108) for the Asian Chicken Stock and optional *kombu.* Substitute 1½ pounds monkfish fillets, cut into ¾-inch cubes, for the chicken breasts.

Shellfish Hot Pot (Yosenabe)

makes 4 to 6 servings

F OR A REALLY striking presentation, place the shucked oysters and clams back into their shells and arrange on the platter. If you wish, add shelled lobster tail, cut into bite-sized pieces, to the assortment.

Ponzu Dipping Sauce (page 122)

4 cups Japanese Sea Stock (page 109) or Asian Fish Stock (page 108)

The Platter (prepared according to the instructions on pages 96-103)

1 pound medium shrimp, peeled and deveined

24 cherrystone or littleneck clams, shucked

12 oysters, shucked

½ pound sea scallops, cut into bite-sized pieces

½ pound squid, cleaned, bodies cut into ¼-inch-thick rounds, tentacles included, if desired

3 cabbage and spinach rolls, cut into rounds, or

8 large outer leaves napa cabbage, cut into 2-inch squares

12 ounces young, tender leaf spinach, tough stems removed

6 scallions, cut into 1½-inch lengths

8 fresh shiitake mushrooms, stems removed, caps cut into ½-inch-thick strips

2 medium carrots, cut on the bias into thin slices, prepared for dipping (see page 14)

Fondue Great Food to Dip, Dunk, Savor, and Swirl

1. Pour the dipping sauce into individual small bowls for dipping.

2. In a large saucepan, bring the stock to a boil over high heat. Transfer to a hot pot or metal fondue pot and keep simmering over a flame.

3. Present the platter. Using chopsticks or small hot pot baskets, allow guests to cook their selections in the simmering broth, and dip them into their own bowl of sauce.

Dessert from a Pot

*I*s there an easier, more wonderful winter dessert than dunking cookies or fresh fruit into warm chocolate fondue? I've never skied, but my winter sports–minded friends often talk about sitting in front of their ski chalet's fireplace with a fondue pot full of chocolate. If that's the reward for a day on cold, wet slopes, I'm willing to try.

There's more to dessert fondues than chocolate—although that's a pretty good start! Fruit fondues are delicious, and should be prepared with flavorful seasonal fruits. Even in the summer, these desserts are as welcoming as warm fruit cobbler (which many of them resemble when served with cookies). I have also included a couple of cheese-based fondues—a sensational mascarpone tiramisù fondue, and a sophisticated triple-crème and Champagne fondue that will turn wonderful strawberries into absolute ambrosia.

It is said that chocolate fondue was invented by the American representatives for the Swiss chocolate bar, Toblerone. In the mid-1960s, they gave a press party that featured Toblerone fondue for dessert. It was a sensation, and found its way onto the menus of many New York restaurants. Next stop was the ski resorts of Europe, then finally Switzerland itself. Talk about culinary trivia . . . by the way, I could not get anyone at Tobler to confirm this story.

Equipment

Chocolate is a delicate ingredient and scorches easily if not protected. The best way to serve chocolate fondue is in a chafing dish (or a fondue set designed to act like a double boiler, with the ceramic pot sitting in the metal one). Otherwise, using a ceramic cheese fondue pot will diffuse the heat and discourage scorching. Do not use a metal fondue pot.

While the flame can be adjusted to very low, sometimes it is best to remove the entire fuel source and replace it with a votive candle. The candle will give off just enough heat to keep the fondue warm yet not enough to cause scorching. The scorching issue isn't such a problem with the other dessert fondues, but they should be kept barely warm over the lowest flame possible.

Ingredients

Chocolate is one of the world's great foods—the cacao tree, whose beans ultimately yield chocolate, didn't get its scientific name, *Theobroma cacao* ("food of the gods"), for nothing. Use the best chocolate you can find, which usually means European. *Bittersweet* (usually European) and *semisweet* (usually American) chocolates are often the same thing. However, European chocolates are usually smoother and have more complex flavor. Recommended brands of European bittersweet chocolate include Lindt, Valrohna, Cacao Barry, and Callebaut. Hershey's Special Dark and Ghirardelli Bittersweet are good American chocolates. *White chocolate* isn't really a chocolate at all, since it doesn't contain any dark cocoa solids and is made from sweetened cocoa butter. My favorite brand is Lindt Blancor. For *milk chocolate,* I use good, old-fashioned Hershey's. Milk chocolate and white chocolate are especially delicate, and must be carefully melted in a double boiler or they will get gritty.

Fondues are probably the simplest desserts a cook can make. When I don't feel like baking from scratch, I simply buy angel food cake, pound cake, or cookies for dipping. It's immaterial to go down a list of dipping cookies, as we all have favorites. Suffice to say that if you think it might taste good dipped in chocolate, it probably will.

Dedicated chocolate lovers may want to indulge their passion by dipping brownies. If you don't think your favorite homemade or bakery-bought brownies will be dense enough to be speared by a fork, try wrapping the brownies in plastic wrap and refrigerating overnight. This trick will turn almost any brownie into a fudgy, chewy delight.

Fruits should be ripe and full of flavor, so think ahead to be sure that they are at their peak when served. For example, if you want to serve peaches, buy them a few days ahead and let them stand out to ripen.

Some people like to include candies as part of their platter. Marshmallows and peppermint sticks are a couple of suggestions. Personally, I prefer baked goods and fruits, but add the candy for variety, if you wish.

Making and Serving Dessert Fondues

As with other fondues, dessert fondues are best made in the kitchen and then transferred to a fondue pot for serving. The pot should be warmed first—fill with very hot tap water, let stand for a few minutes, then pour out the water and dry the pot. As mentioned above, be sure that the heating flame is gentle, especially with chocolate fondues.

Dessert fondues include sugar, which gets hot and stays hot. One advantage of a gentle flame is that the fondue will cool to a safe temperature, and not remain piping hot.

Classic Chocolate Fondue

makes 4 to 6 servings

SIMPLE, YES . . . BUT sublime. The chosen chocolate will dictate the outcome, so pick the one that makes you sigh when you nibble it in its plain, unadorned glory. There are many variations to be had on the theme of chocolate and cream in a fondue pot, so let your personal taste be your guide. Kahlúa, Amaretto, Frangelico, Coco Rico, Grand Marnier (with or without orange zest), kirschwasser, dark rum, or bourbon are just a few "spirited" suggestions for flavoring the fondue. If you prefer to delete the alcohol, spike the fondue with one of the many appropriate coffee syrups available for sale at coffee bars or gourmet stores.

¾ cup heavy cream

12 ounces high-quality bittersweet chocolate, finely chopped

1 to 2 tablespoons Cognac, brandy, or liqueur

What to Dip

Pound cake, cut into bite-sized cubes • Large, fresh strawberries, with stems attached • Fresh cherries, pitted • Fresh clementines, peeled and divided into sections • Fresh pineapple, pared, cored, and cut into bite-sized wedges • Dried apricots • Glazed oranges, cut into wedges

1. In a medium, heavy-bottomed saucepan, heat the cream until very hot. Add the chocolate and let stand until softened, about 3 minutes. Add the Cognac and whisk until smooth.

continued

2. Transfer to a ceramic fondue pot or ceramic chafing dish and keep warm over a burner. Serve immediately, with the dipping ingredients of your choice.

Chocolate-Orange Fondue: Stir the grated zest of 1 orange and 2 tablespoons orange-flavored liqueur, such as Grand Marnier into the fondue.

Black Forest Fondue: Stir 2 tablespoons finely chopped, cherry preserves and 2 tablespoons kirsch into the fondue.

Chocolate-Raspberry Fondue: Stir 2 tablespoons Chambord (black raspberry liqueur) into the fondue.

Chocolate Mint Fondue: Stir 1 or 2 tablespoons crème de menthe liqueur into the fondue.

Chocolate-Coconut-Almond Fondue

THE COMBINATION OF milk chocolate, coconut, and almonds has put a smile on many a person's face, usually in the form of a Mounds candy bar—this fondue is a tribute to this terrific trio.

½ cup sliced almonds

1 cup cream of coconut, such as Coco Lopez

½ cup heavy cream

12 ounces high-quality milk chocolate, finely chopped

1 ounce unsweetened chocolate, finely chopped

½ cup desiccated coconut flakes

What to Dip

Pound cake, cut into bite-sized cubes • Angel food cake, cut into bite-sized cubes • Large, whole strawberries with stems attached • Bananas, cut into bite-sized pieces

1. Position a rack in the top third of the oven and preheat to 350°F. Spread the almonds on a baking sheet. Bake, stirring occasionally, until the almonds are toasted, about 8 minutes. Cool completely. Chop the almonds finely and set aside.

2. In a medium, heavy-bottomed saucepan, bring the cream of coconut and heavy cream to a simmer over medium heat. Remove from the heat and add the chocolates. Let stand until the chocolates soften, about 3 minutes. Whisk until smooth.

3. Transfer to a ceramic fondue pot or chafing dish and keep warm over a burner. Serve immediately with the dipping ingredients and bowls of the almonds and coconut. Allow guests to sprinkle their dipped food with the almonds and coconut before eating.

Venetian Espresso Fondue

makes 4 to 6 servings

SAN FRANCISCO, MY home town, is known for its cool, foggy nights. But San Franciscans know a great warmer-upper: go to North Beach's Café Tosca and order a Venetian Coffee—hot chocolate with a shot of espresso and another shot of brandy. Here's that San Franciscan treat, but in a fondue pot. I serve it with all different kinds of Italian cookies, but it's also very good with pound cake.

> **What to Dip**
>
> Assorted Italian cookies •
> Pound cake, cut into
> bite-sized cubes

½ cup water

¼ cup plus 2 tablespoons heavy cream

5 teaspoons instant espresso powder (see Note, page 147)

2 tablespoons confectioners' sugar, plus more to taste

12 ounces high-quality bittersweet chocolate, finely chopped

2 tablespoons brandy

1. In a medium, heavy-bottomed saucepan, bring the water and heavy cream to a boil over high heat. Remove from the heat and stir in the espresso powder and 2 tablespoons confectioners' sugar until dissolved.

2. Add the chocolate and let stand until softened, about 3 minutes. Add the brandy and whisk until smooth. Taste, and add additional sugar, if desired (the exact amount depends on the chocolate brand).

3. Transfer to a ceramic fondue pot and keep warm over a burner. Serve immediately with the dipping ingredients.

Continental
Candy Bar Fondue

makes 6 to 8 servings

D URING MY FIRST trip to Switzerland, I had a
Swiss milk chocolate candy bar filled with a creamy
orange–Grand Marnier filling. I was so love-struck, I wanted
to fill my suitcase with them. (The American versions are
demurely alcohol-free.) Back home, I was happy to discover
these bars make a great chocolate fondue that takes on the flavor of the filling. My favorite is made with the orange bars, but
there are many other possibilities.
Try the raspberry bars with Chambord liqueur, hazelnut with Frangelico,
or pistachio with Amaretto.

¾ cup heavy cream

4 (3½-ounce) orange-filled milk

chocolate candy bars

2 teaspoons orange-flavored

liqueur, such as Grand Marnier

What to Dip

Your favorite cookies,
preferably small, elegant
ones from a French-style
bakery • Clementines,
peeled and divided into
sections • Large, whole
strawberries with stems
attached

1. In a small saucepan, over medium heat, bring the cream to
a simmer. Transfer to the top part of a double boiler set over
medium heat.

2. Working over the double boiler, break up the chocolate bars
into pieces, and let the pieces fall into the hot cream. Try to
make them as small as you can, but don't be compulsive about
it. Let the chocolate stand until softened, about 3 minutes. Add
the liqueur and whisk until smooth.

continued

3. Transfer to a ceramic fondue pot or chafing dish and keep warm over a burner. Serve immediately, with the dipping ingredients of your choice.

Peanut Butter and Milk Chocolate Fondue

makes 4 to 6 servings

FOR KIDS OF all ages, here's a fondue with the All-American flavors of peanuts and milk chocolate. Whenever I serve this sinful fondue to self-controlled, respectable grownups, they tend to regress, in a somewhat embarrassing manner, into greedy little children.

What to Dip

Pretzels or pretzel sticks • Brownies, cut into bite-sized pieces • Bananas, cut into bite-sized pieces

1 cup heavy cream

6 ounces milk chocolate, finely chopped

½ cup chunky peanut butter

1. In a small saucepan over medium heat, heat the cream until simmering. Transfer to the top part of a double boiler set over simmering heat. Add the milk chocolate and let stand until softened, about 1 minute. Whisk until melted. Gradually whisk in the peanut butter until the fondue is smooth.

2. Transfer to a ceramic fondue pot or chafing dish and keep warm over a burner. Serve immediately with the dipping ingredients of your choice.

The Original
Toblerone Fondue

makes 4 servings

Here it is, the fondue heard round the world. The crunchy bits of nougat and hazelnuts in the Toblerone bar really do add something to this chocolate fondue. The original recipe (circa 1966) calls for Cognac, but lately I use the hazelnut liqueur, Frangelico, or even hazelnut-flavored coffee syrup.

²/₃ cup heavy cream

4 (3½-ounce) bars Toblerone, finely chopped

1 tablespoon Cognac or Frangelico liqueur

What to Dip

Pound cake, cut into bite-sized cubes • Angel food cake, cut into bite-sized cubes • Large, whole strawberries with stems • Ripe peaches or nectarines, pitted and sliced • Bananas, cut into bite-sized pieces

1. In a medium, heavy-bottomed saucepan, bring the cream to a simmer over medium heat. Remove from the heat and add the chopped Toblerone bars. Let stand until the Toblerone softens, about 3 minutes. Add the Cognac and whisk until smooth.

2. Transfer to a ceramic fondue pot or chafing dish and keep warm over a burner. Serve immediately, with the dipping ingredients of your choice.

White Chocolate and Raspberry Swirl Fondue

makes 6 to 8 servings

R ED RASPBERRY PURÉE swirled into ivory white chocolate creates a show-stopping, marbleized look. Also, the acidic raspberries help to balance the sugariness of the white chocolate. Because of white chocolate's inherent sweetness, I prefer to serve this with tart fruits or not-too-sweet cookies, like biscotti.

1 (6-ounce) basket fresh
raspberries

1 cup heavy cream

1 pound high-quality white
chocolate, finely chopped

What to Dip

Biscotti • Large, whole strawberries, with stems attached • Ripe peaches or nectarines, pitted and sliced • Raspberries • Bananas, cut into bite-sized pieces • Ripe pineapple, pared, cored, and cut into bite-sized wedges

1. Set aside about one-third of the raspberries for dipping into the finished fondue. In a blender or a food processor fitted with the metal chopping blade, purée the remaining raspberries. Strain the purée through a fine-meshed wire sieve into a small bowl, rubbing the purée through the sieve with a rubber spatula. Discard the seeds. Set the strained purée aside.

2. In a medium, heavy-bottomed saucepan, bring the cream to a simmer over medium heat. Remove from the heat and add the white chocolate. Let stand until the chocolate softens, about 3 minutes. Whisk until smooth.

3. Transfer the fondue to a ceramic fondue pot or chafing dish and keep warm over a burner. Drizzle the raspberry purée over

the fondue. Swirl a knife through the purée to create a marbleized effect. Serve immediately, with the reserved raspberries and other ingredients of your choice for dipping.

Double-Berry and Riesling Fondue

makes 4 to 6 servings

SUMMERTIME COOKING SHOULD be easy, using fruits at their seasonal peaks. You'll be hard pressed when deciding how to use this fondue—while it is a great dipping fondue for pound cake and cookies, it is also a superb ice cream topping.

1 pint fresh blueberries

2 (6-ounce) baskets fresh raspberries

½ cup fruity, semi-dry white wine, such as Riesling

½ cup less 1 tablespoon sugar

1 tablespoon plus 1 teaspoon cornstarch

1½ tablespoons fresh lemon juice

What to Dip

Angel food cake, cut into bite-sized cubes • Pound cake, cut into bite-sized cubes • Ladyfingers, either the soft French variety or crisp Italian *savoiardi* • Large, whole strawberries, with stems attached • Cherries, pitted • Ripe apricots, pitted, cut into wedges • Ripe peaches or nectarines, pitted, cut into wedges, tossed with lemon juice to discourage browning

1. In a food processor fitted with the metal blade, process the blueberries and raspberries until puréed. Pour the purée into a

sieve set over a medium bowl. Using a rubber spatula, rub as much purée as possible through the sieve, discarding the seeds and skin left behind in the sieve. You should have about 1⅔ cups seedless puree.

2. In a medium, nonreactive saucepan, bring the purée, wine, and sugar to a simmer over medium heat, stirring often to dissolve the sugar. Reduce the heat to medium-low and simmer for 5 minutes. In a small bowl, dissolve the cornstarch in the lemon juice. Stir into the berry mixture and cook until thickened.

3. Transfer to a ceramic fondue pot or chafing dish and keep warm over a burner. Serve immediately, with the dipping ingredients of your choice.

Fresh Cherries Jubilee Fondue

makes 4 to 6 servings

CHERRIES JUBILEE IS another one of those classic dishes that is making a comeback—it's too bad that most versions use canned cherries. You can serve this version in the traditional manner, spooned over ice cream, or as a dip for bite-sized cake cubes or fruit. Bing cherries, hard to beat for eating out of hand, lose a little flavor when heated, so give them a boost with the addition of high-quality cherry preserves.

Sweet and Tart Lemon Fondue

makes 4 to 6 servings

ONE OF MY favorite desserts is lemon tart—tangy lemon curd spread into a sweet pastry shell—and my favorite part of making it is licking the warm curd off the spoon. This fondue allows me to enjoy this sensation by the potful. Carry the "tart" motif further by dipping shortbread cookies, which resemble a sweet tart crust.

What to Dip

Large, whole strawberries, with stems attached • Shortbread cookies

1½ cups water

¾ cup sugar

3 tablespoons cornstarch

6 tablespoons (½ stick plus 2 tablespoons) unsalted butter, chilled and cut into pieces

⅓ cup fresh lemon juice

3 large egg yolks

Zest of 1 lemon

1. In a medium, heavy-bottomed saucepan, combine the water and sugar. Sprinkle the cornstarch over the top and whisk to dissolve. Bring to a simmer over medium heat, whisking often. Remove from the heat and whisk in the butter, then the lemon juice.

2. In a small bowl, whisk the egg yolks. Gradually add about ½ cup of the hot lemon juice mixture to the yolks. Stir the yolk mixture into the saucepan. Stirring constantly, bring to a simmer over medium heat.

1 pound fresh Bing cherries,
  pitted and coarsely chopped

½ cup cherry preserves,
  preferably imported

½ cup sugar

1 tablespoon fresh lemon juice

¼ cup water

2 teaspoons cornstarch

2 tablespoons kirsch, cherry schnapps, or Cognac

What to Dip

Chocolate pound cake, cut
into bite-sized cubes •
Angel food cake, cut into
bite-sized cubes

1. In a medium, heavy-bottomed saucepan, bring the cherries, cherry preserves, sugar, lemon juice, and water to a simmer over medium heat, stirring to dissolve the sugar. Reduce the heat to low and cover. Simmer until the cherries give off their juices, about 8 minutes. In a small bowl, dissolve the cornstarch in the kirsch. Stir into the fondue and cook until thickened.

2. Transfer to a ceramic fondue pot or chafing dish and keep warm over a burner. Serve immediately, with the dipping ingredients of your choice.

3. Strain into a ceramic fondue pot or chafing dish (straining will remove any stray bits of coagulated egg white). Stir in the zest. Serve immediately, with the dipping ingredients of your choice.

Peach Caramel Fondue

makes 6 to 8 servings

WHEN SUMMER PEACHES are in season and bursting with flavor, try this fondue. On the other hand, if your peaches aren't as tasty as they should be, use thawed frozen peaches—you may be surprised to find they are a very high-quality product, and, unfortunately, are often more reliable than the fresh ones.

4 ripe, medium peaches (1½ pounds)

1 tablespoon fresh lemon juice

¼ cup plus 2 tablespoons heavy cream

4 tablespoons (½ stick) unsalted butter, cut into pieces

¾ cup packed light brown sugar

1 tablespoon plus 1 teaspoon cornstarch

3 tablespoons bourbon, dark rum, or apple juice

What to Dip

Pound cake, cut into bite-sized cubes • Angel food cake, cut into bite-sized cubes • Large, whole strawberries with stems attached • Peaches or nectarines, pitted and sliced • Bananas, cut into bite-sized pieces

1. Bring a large pot of water to a boil over high heat. Add the peaches and cook until the skins loosen, 30 to 60 seconds depending on the ripeness of the peaches. Using a slotted spoon, transfer the peaches to a bowl of iced water and let stand until cool enough to handle. Peel the peaches, remove the pits, and coarsely chop the flesh. In a blender or a food processor fitted with the metal blade, purée the peaches with the lemon juice. You should have 1¾ cups.

2. In a medium, heavy-bottomed saucepan, bring ¼ cup of the cream and the butter to a simmer over medium heat, stirring often to melt the butter. Add the brown sugar and stir until dissolved. Reduce the heat to low and simmer for 5 minutes.

3. Stir in the peach purée and bring to a simmer. In a small bowl, dissolve the cornstarch in the bourbon. Stir into the saucepan and cook until thickened.

4. Transfer to a ceramic fondue pot or chafing dish and keep warm over a burner. Drizzle the remaining 2 tablespoons heavy cream over the top of the fondue. Serve immediately, with the dipping ingredients of your choice.

Triple-Crème and Champagne Fondue

makes 4 servings

IF THERE IS anything more wonderful than this creamy fondue for dipping strawberries, I haven't found it. Well, okay, maybe one of the chocolate fondues. But when you want a very special, not-too-sweet *cheese* fondue to serve with Champagne for a celebration meal, look no further. This recipe makes a modest amount, but it is very rich and can be easily doubled.

¾ cup good-quality French
   Champagne or California
   sparkling wine
2 tablespoons confectioners'
   sugar
1 tablespoon lemon juice
1 pound ripe Explorateur or
   other triple-crème cheese,
   well chilled, rind removed,
   and cut into small bite-sized cubes (2½ cups)
1 tablespoon cornstarch
1 tablespoon Cognac

What to Dip

Ladyfingers, either the soft French variety or the crisp Italian *savoiardi* • Large strawberries with the stems attached • Seedless grapes • Peaches, pitted and sliced • Dried apricots

1. In a medium, heavy-bottomed saucepan, bring the Champagne, confectioners' sugar, and lemon juice to a bare simmer over medium heat.

2. In a medium bowl, mash the cheese and cornstarch together with a rubber spatula until well combined. In two or three batches, stir the cheese into the saucepan, stirring until the first addition is melted before adding another. Stir in the Cognac.

3. Transfer to a ceramic fondue pot or chafing dish and keep warm over a burner. Serve immediately, with the dipping ingredients of your choice.

Tiramisù Mascarpone Fondue

makes 4 to 6 servings

THE WORLD HAS fallen in love with tiramisù—the Venetian dessert of ladyfingers, espresso, and mascarpone cheese. Here, I've made a sweet cheese fondue for dipping crisp Italian ladyfingers (*savoiardi,* available at Italian food stores) and summer fruit like juicy strawberries and peaches. There are a couple of things to watch out for in this recipe. First, use sweet, not dry, Marsala wine—the dry is used only for savory dishes, and this is a dessert. Also, be sure not to overcook the mixture once the egg yolks have been added, or the yolks will curdle. An instant-read thermometer will help gauge the right temperature.

What to Dip

Crisp Italian ladyfingers (*savoiardi*) • Large, whole strawberries, with stems attached • Ripe peaches, cut into wedges

1 teaspoon instant espresso powder (see Note)

1 tablespoon boiling water

1 (17-ounce) container mascarpone cheese

¼ cup confectioners' sugar

2 tablespoons sweet Marsala wine

2 teaspoons cornstarch

3 large egg yolks, at room temperature

Finely chopped bittersweet chocolate, for serving

1. In a small bowl, dissolve the espresso powder in the boiling water. In the top part of a double boiler over simmering water, combine the espresso liquid, the mascarpone, confectioners'

sugar, Marsala, and cornstarch, mashing with a rubber spatula until the mascarpone has melted and the mixture is smooth.

2. In a medium bowl, whisk the egg yolks to combine. Gradually whisk in about ½ cup of the warm mascarpone mixture. Whisk the egg yolk mixture into the mascarpone mixture. Whisking constantly, cook until the fondue is hot and thickened (an instant-read thermometer will read 180°F.), about 2 minutes.

3. Transfer to a ceramic fondue pot or chafing dish and keep warm over a burner. Place the chopped chocolate in small, individual bowls. Serve immediately, with the dipping ingredients of your choice, allowing guests to dip their fondue-covered food in the chocolate before eating.

Note: Instant espresso powder is available at Italian food stores and many supermarkets. If necessary, substitute 1½ teaspoons regular instant coffee powder, but it won't have the espresso's deep-roasted flavor.

Index